STRENGTH AND ALLIANCE

CHURCH MILITANT
FIELD JOURNAL

First Edition, 2013

ISBN: 0615760724

ISBN-13: 978-0615760728

Deus Vult Press

3673 County Highway P

Cross Plains, WI 53528

For additional Search and Rescue Journal pages, Prayer Request Journal pages, and Church Militant Boot Camp Journal pages, visit *churchmilitant.com*

STRENGTH AND ALLIANCE

CHURCH MILITANT FIELD JOURNAL

BY FR. RICHARD M. HEILMAN

CONTENTS

INTRODUCTION

Let's Roll

This is a clarion call to raise an army willing to *"fight for the souls"* of our loved ones. All around us we see one soul after another losing their precious gift of faith. Most of us feel helpless to do anything about it. Our ancestors knew exactly what to do, but the modern Christian has lost the ancient art of "fighting for souls."

This is a companion field journal to the *Church Militant Field Manual*. In this field journal you will find a year's worth of pages available for keeping record of all your Church Militant training and missions. You will find a Search and Rescue journal that will help you build your own personal army of intercessors by praying for the holy souls and invoking the saints. This personal Holy Alliance will then assist you in rescuing the souls of your living loved ones who are captivated by the world and have lost the gift of faith.

Also, you will find a Church Militant Boot Camp journal. A boot camp trains soldiers for combat by instilling discipline and an unbreakable bond. When training is complete, soldiers act more as a sacrificing, corporate body and less as self-concerned individuals. You will learn what it means to be God Strong, under His power of grace, and how absolutely essential it is to move in concert, in alliance with the Communion of Saints.

During this Church Militant Boot Camp you will learn the following:

✠ The fundamentals of a quality interior life.

✠ What it means to be commissioned as an officer in the Church Militant.

✠ How to become not just Army Strong but God Strong in the power of His grace.

✠ How to build your own personal army of intercessors by praying for the holy souls and invoking the saints.

✠ The value of the Warrior Ethos: "I will never leave a fallen comrade." Many of our living loved ones are captivated by the world and have lost the gift of faith, and our deceased loved ones wait with longing for our prayers to help them reach heaven.

This is no ordinary army, and therefore, this will be no ordinary training. What is more, we must bear in mind that this is no ordinary adversary we face.

Let's recall St. Paul's exhortation:

"Be strong in the Lord and in His mighty power. Put on the full armor of God, so that you can take your stand against the devil's schemes. For our struggle is not against flesh and blood but against the rulers, against the authorities, against the powers of this dark world, and against the spiritual forces of evil in the heavenly realms" (Eph 6:10-12).

LET'S ROLL!

"I've Got Your Six!"

"The fervent petition of a holy man is powerful indeed. My brothers, the case may arise among you of someone straying from the truth and of another bringing him back. Remember this: the person who brings a sinner back from his way will save his soul from death and cancel a multitude of sins" (Jas 5:16b, 19-20).

"I've got your six" is a military phrase that basically means "I've got your back." It comes from the old pilot system in which directions correspond to hours on the clock, where 12 o'clock is forward and 6 o'clock is behind. Thus anyone behind you is "at your six."

Blessed Peter Favre said, "I felt great desires that the saints might pray for us, they who have so much power in their state of glory, and that the souls in purgatory might offer prayers for us amidst those remorseful lamentations of theirs ... these souls can do much for us (more than we can tell)." St. John Vianney said, "Oh! If all of us but knew how great is the power of the good souls in purgatory with the heart of God, and if we knew all the graces we can attain through their intercession, they would not be so much forgotten! We must pray much for them, so that they may pray much for us."

We are not meant to advance unaided. In His great wisdom, God has set up a Holy Alliance that, once united, is designed to defeat any and all forces of darkness in the heavenly realm, rescue souls, and build up the kingdom of God. This alliance is called the Communion of Saints, and is comprised of the Church Militant (those alive on earth), the Church Penitent (those undergoing purification in purgatory in preparation for heaven), and the Church Triumphant (those already in heaven). It is the exchange of the *Sancta Sanctis!* ("God's holy gifts for God's holy people!") Those on earth (Church Militant) invoke the saints in heaven and pray for the souls in purgatory (we

9

can gain indulgences for them). When called upon, those in heaven pray for the Church Militant and the Church Penitent; they obtain graces for us on earth and an alleviation of suffering for the poor souls in purgatory. Those in purgatory can, when called upon, invoke the saints on high and pray for us struggling with the world, the flesh, and the evil spirit.

St. Thomas Aquinas wrote: "Charity is incomplete until it includes the dead as well as the living." While we live together on earth as Christians, we are in communion, or unity, with one another. But that communion doesn't end when one of us dies. In the Communion of Saints "a perennial link of charity exists between the faithful who have already reached their heavenly home, those who are expiating their sins in purgatory, and those who are still pilgrims on earth. Between them there is, too, an abundant exchange of all good things."[1] In other words, the bond of love remains, along with the self-emptying nature of that real love. Even separated by death, we continue to care for each other, look out for each other, and build each other up. And so we continue to say to one another, "I've got your six!"

To understand how God's amazing structure for this loving exchange of spiritual goods is built, we must learn what we mean by indulgences. St. Ignatius of Loyola wrote, "Indulgences are of such value that I find myself unable to appreciate them according to their true worth or to speak of them highly enough. Thus I exhort you to hold them in the highest possible esteem."

Indulgences 101

In the last days of Pope John Paul II's pontificate, he met with some American bishops in May of 2004 and recommended that U.S. Catholics recover "devotions of popular piety" as a means of "personal and communal sanctification."[2] Sadly, many wonderful Catholic devotional treasures had been discarded, by and large, during the rebellious days following the Council of Vatican II. But, by the grace of God, the practice of gaining indulgences for ourselves and the holy souls in purgatory is being restored.

Catholic Answers' *Primer on Indulgences* teaches:

"Those who claim that indulgences are no longer part of Church teaching have the admirable desire to distance themselves from abuses that occurred around the time of the Protestant Reformation. They also want to remove stumbling blocks that prevent non-Catholics from taking a positive view of the Church. As admirable as these motives are, the claim that indulgences are not part of Church teaching today is false. This is proved by the Catechism of the Catholic Church, which states, 'An indulgence is obtained through the Church who, by virtue of the power of binding and loosing granted her by Christ Jesus, intervenes in favor of individual Christians and opens for them the treasury of the merits of Christ and the saints to obtain from the Father of mercies the remission of the temporal punishment due for their sins.' The Church does this not just to aid Christians, 'but also to spur them to works of devotion, penance, and charity' (CCC 1478)."[3]

What is an indulgence? The word comes from the Latin *indulgentia*, which means "to be kind or tender." "To understand what an indulgence is," writes contemporary author Steve Kellmeyer, "we have to know what our sin does to the world and ourselves. When we commit sin, two things happen. First, we kill the life of grace within us. This deserves punishment. Spiritually, a sinner is a dead man, walking. Second, by removing grace from ourselves, we also remove grace from the created universe. Thus, each sin, no matter how venial, attacks both the moral order of the universe and the very material of creation itself."[4]

The following explanation of indulgences comes from Steve Kellmeyer's *Calendar of Indulgences*:

"**Forgiveness:** When God pours out mercy in the Sacrament of Reconciliation, He does something we have no right to expect — He forgives our sins and restores the life of grace within us, resurrecting us from death. As a result, we must act (penance) to change our life and renew our way of living (amendment of life). However, though we have been resurrected, we still deserve punishment for the attack we made on God's creation. Further, the horrible consequences of our attack, which removed grace from creation, continue to affect the world even if we ourselves have been healed through the sacrament. God expects us to help repair the damage.

"**Repair Work:** We can do this repair work either here on earth or in purgatory. Since God intended us to live with our bodies united to our souls, it is much easier to do this repair work here. In purgatory, our soul and body are separate. The suffering of purgatory is always much more painful than suffering on earth because it is harder to do the necessary repair work when the body isn't around to help.

"**The Storehouse:** Cardinal John Newman said, 'The smallest venial sin rocks the foundations of the created world.' That is, even our smallest sin can cause devastating consequences in creation; famine, disease, natural disaster. However, through God's grace, the holiness of even the lowliest saint far exceeds the harm even the greatest sinner can do. Further, Christ's work on the cross is infinitely greater in merit than that of the greatest saint in Christendom, the Blessed Virgin Mary. Thus, the graces won by Christ and the saints are an infinite treasure that can be used to heal the wounds of the world. God intends us to use this treasury — indeed; we could not help wipe out the effects of our sin without the divine treasury God established. *An indulgence, then, applies the graces won by Christ and the saints to the world so as to heal the wounds I caused by my sins.*

"A plenary indulgence heals all of the effects of one person's sins. A partial indulgence heals part of the effects. One can win indulgences only for oneself or those in purgatory who have need of assistance because they currently lack bodies. Indulgences cannot be applied towards other living persons. Every living person is supposed to do his own acts of obedience to help heal the worldly effects of his own sinfulness (CCC 1471-1473)."[5]

Requirements for obtaining a plenary indulgence:

✠ Do the work while in a state of grace
✠ Receive sacramental Confession within 20 days of the work (several plenary indulgences may be earned per reception)
✠ Receive Eucharistic communion (one plenary indulgence may be earned per reception of Eucharist)
✠ Pray for the pope's intentions (an Our Father and Hail Mary, or other appropriate prayer, is sufficient)
✠ Have no attachment to sin (even venial) — i.e., the Christian makes an act of the will to love God and despise sin

Requirements for obtaining a partial indulgence:

✠ Do the work while in a state of grace
✠ Have the general intention of earning an indulgence

Spiritual Strength Conditioning

"No other labor is as difficult as prayer to God. Every time a person wants to pray, our spiritual enemies want to come and disrupt it, for they know that it is only by deflecting humans from prayer that they can do them any harm." - Abba Agathon, 4th century.

While Holy Mother Church unlocks her spiritual treasury she, like any good mother, utilizes these prescribed acts of obedience as an occasion to teach her children ("spurs us to works of devotion, penance, and charity" CCC 1478). In other words, when we look at each of the indulgenced good works and prayers granted to us, as well as the conditions necessary for obtaining them, we see that these acts and conditions are the favored ways in which God desires us to grow in holiness, confront evil, and rescue souls.

Consider the conditions required for obtaining a plenary indulgence. If our state in life allows it, the ideal is to obtain one plenary indulgence every day (Mother Church offers one plenary indulgence, and only one, each day). By setting the following conditions, Holy Mother Church is teaching that these conditions reveal what is a rock solid foundation for the interior life:

✠ Sustain and guard your state of grace

✠ Go to Confession frequently (at least once a month)

✠ Hear Daily Mass and receive Communion

✠ Prayer support for our leader (pope)

✠ Free from the slavery of unresolved sin

Like athletes or soldiers dedicated to their training, these "conditions" are our way of maintaining sound spiritual strength conditioning, empowering us to be the qualified contenders God can trust for His missions to battle dark forces and rescue souls. Apart from these basic "conditions," we are weak and vulnerable and God is unlikely to choose us for His missions or bless our endeavors. We are, in essence, sidelined (benched) until we desire to choose His fundamental conditions to get in good spiritual shape.

By elevating certain prayers and good works to the level of gaining an indulgence, Mother Church is identifying which of these she most highly values and, therefore, which ones she urges us to prioritize. This is the best way for us to practice sincere obedience. These indulgenced prayers and good works are all listed in the *Manual of Indulgences* (and easily accessible online).

The 'Big Four'

However, we must draw special attention to what I call the "Big Four." Remarkably, Holy Mother Church has elevated only four activities for which a plenary indulgence can be gained on any day (though, as we said, only once a day). Highlighting these four reveals the great esteem in which Mother Church holds them, and, therefore, she urges us to rank these as highest among our daily devotions. The "Big Four" are:

✠ Adoring the Blessed Sacrament for at least 30 minutes

✠ Devoutly reading Sacred Scripture for at least 30 minutes

✠ Devoutly performing the Stations of the Cross

✠ Reciting the Rosary with members of the family, or in a church, oratory, religious community, or pious association

The great significance of the "Big Four" is that Mother Church has provided a way for us to gain that one plenary indulgence every day for ourselves or for a poor soul in purgatory. This then raises the question: Why would we squander this incredibly generous gift? Why wouldn't we accept Mother Church's gracious provision and seek this plenary indulgence every day?

Building Your Holy Alliance

How many of us had grandparents who had their stack of holy cards in their prayer book? These favorite saints were their friends, their prayer warriors! How many of our ancestors knew to pray for the holy souls in purgatory, especially the souls of family and friends? The holy souls would then, in deep gratitude, return many prayers for those who cared to pray for them. This is why our ancestors never faced evil alone or prayed for anything or anybody alone — they had their comrades in the heavenly realm, their Holy Alliance of saints and holy souls, with them at all times. The devil never stood a chance against this united force!

What's stopping us from building upon the great example of our ancestors who called upon the saints to pray with them for the poor souls in purgatory? If they invoked (recruited) their handful of favorite saints, what's stopping us from building an enormous personal Holy Alliance of saints (as we learn about each one) by recruiting a new saint each day to pray with us? And, while our ancestors had a handful of deceased family and friends for whom they prayed, what's stopping us from going deeper in our family tree (as we learn about each one) by helping more and more generations of our family to reach heaven? These deceased relatives and friends (holy souls) would also be considered recruits in our Holy Alliance as they become "very grateful" holy souls who now pray for us because we prayed for them.

There is something special about invoking (recruiting) each of these saints and holy souls *mano-a-mano* (hand to hand — to give it in person) as opposed to a general calling out for "all the saints" or "all the holy souls." The former is a more loving and personal act of reaching out to each saint and holy soul as we get to know him or her.

The latter tends toward more of an impersonal, face-in-the-crowd relationship.

This means that on day one that you begin this practice of praying with a saint for a holy soul in purgatory, you grow from a force of one (just you) to a force of three (the saint you chose, the holy soul you prayed for, and you). On day two, you will add another saint and holy soul to your personal Holy Alliance, and grow to a force of five. And so on.

Different units and formations organize the military. It's interesting to think that, as our Holy Alliance grows, it will be akin to these units:

Your Holy Alliance:

Fire team:	2-4
Squad:	8-13
Platoon:	26-55
Company:	80-225
Battalion:	300-1,300
Regiment:	3,000-5,000
Division:	10,000-15,000

Think about it — inside of six months, you can grow your Holy Alliance to the size of a battalion. Imagine standing before the throne of God, calling out to Him on behalf of a loved one who has lost the precious gift of faith. But now, you do not stand alone — you are standing there with your personal battalion "at your six." Amazing!

Store up Spiritual Energy

The heroes of our faith are the warrior saints who have gone before us. God worked mightily and miraculously through them. Therefore, we must study their ways. In humility, obedience, and trust (H.O.T.), we ask: How did they remain so well connected, in such strong friendship with God, so that His river of supernatural grace could flow so freely through them? What do these "SEALS for Christ" teach us about the ideal spiritual disciplines, the ultimate daily regimen of prayer?

"Pray with great confidence," St. Louis de Montfort says, "with confidence based upon the goodness and infinite generosity of God and upon the promises of Jesus Christ. God is a spring of living water that flows unceasingly into the hearts of those who pray."

Prayer is our outstanding supernatural resource for fighting the wiles of the enemy. St. Alphonsus said, "Prayer is, beyond doubt, the most powerful weapon the Lord gives us to conquer evil ... but we must really put ourselves into the prayer, it is not enough just to say the words, it must come from the heart. And also prayer needs to be continuous, we must pray no matter what kind of situation we find ourselves in: the warfare we are engaged in is ongoing, so our prayer must be on-going also."

The following are largely based on Fr. John McCloskey's *Seven Daily Habits of Holy Apostolic People* and include:

1. The Morning Offering
2. Mental Prayer (at least 15 minutes)
3. Spiritual Reading (at least 15 minutes)
4. Holy Mass and Communion
5. The Angelus (at noon)
6. The Holy Rosary
7. Brief Examination of Conscience (at night)

Father McCloskey writes: "These are the principal means to achieve holiness. If you are a person who wants to bring Christ to others through your friendship, these are the instruments by which you store up the spiritual energy that will enable you to do so. Apostolic action without the sacraments and a deep solid interior life will in the long run be ineffective. You can be sure that all the saints incorporated in one way or another all of these habits into their daily routine. Your goal is to be like them, contemplatives in the middle of the world."[6]

We are being asked to allow God's grace to surge through us to a waiting world, but *nemo dat quod non habet* (no one gives what he does not have). Father McCloskey correctly points out that these exceptional habits of prayer are the way of *storing up spiritual energy* to be used to bring Christ to others. St. Bernadette said: "Do not just be a channel for grace, but a reservoir, an overflowing reservoir. No sooner has a channel received grace than it pours it out. A reservoir waits to be filled up and then offers grace to those who come to draw from its superabundance."

Let's consider some key points before we look more closely at each of these seven daily habits:

First, just like someone who is starting a daily exercise program, you don't go out and run several miles on the first day. That would invite failure, and God wants to see you succeed. Take it easy on yourself as you incorporate these habits in your daily routine over time. Consider using the Church Militant Boot Camp Journal starting on page 115 as a very effective way to get your robust interior life up and running.

Second, while gradually implementing these habits, you still want to make a firm commitment, with the help of the Holy Spirit, to make them *the* priority in your life — more important than meals, sleep, work, and recreation.

Third, St. Basil writes, "The reason why sometimes you have asked and not received is because you have asked amiss, either inconsistently, or lightly, or because you have asked for what was not good for you, or because you have ceased asking." It is time to set aside the undisciplined, "free-styling" way in which most of us have practiced our daily prayer life throughout our lives. The *cult of the casual* has become so pervasive in the world that it has seeped into our faith lives. This lack of discipline has spelled disaster for those who have ever attempted to maintain regular habits of prayer. These habits must be done when we are most alert, during the day, in a place that is silent and without distractions, where it is easy to put ourselves in God's presence and address Him. Schedule your prayer or it will never happen.

Fourth, Father McCloskey points out that "living the seven daily habits is not a zero sum game. You are not losing time but rather, in reality, gaining it. I have never met a person who lived them on a daily basis who became a less productive worker as a result, or a worse spouse, or who had less time for his friends, or could no longer grow in his cultural life. Quite the contrary, God always rewards those who put Him first. Our Lord will multiply our time amazingly as He did with those few loaves and fishes that fed the multitude with plenty left over."[7]

1. Morning Offering: This is a prayer that lets you begin by offering up your entire day for the glory of God. St. Josemaria Escriva also encourages us to get up on the dot: "Conquer yourself each day from the very first moment, getting up on the dot, at a set time, without granting a single minute to laziness. If with the help of God, you conquer yourself in the moment, you have accomplished a great deal for the rest of the day. It's so discouraging to find yourself beaten in the first skirmish."[8] This is called the "heroic moment" and gives us the physical and spiritual energy throughout the day to stop what we are doing in order to live the other habits. Once your feet hit the ground, speak the words "I will serve!" (or *Serviam*, in Latin).

2. **Mental Prayer (15 minutes):** This is "face time," the "one thing necessary" *(unum necessarium)* that constitutes the essential foundation for the interior life. This prayer is simply one-on-one direct conversation with Jesus Christ, preferably before the Blessed Sacrament in the tabernacle.

3. **Spiritual Reading (15 minutes):** This refers to the systematic reading of Sacred Scripture known as Lectio Divina as well as the classic understanding of spiritual reading that is devoted to the reading of lives of saints, writings of Doctors and the Fathers of the Church, and other works written by holy people. As St. Josemaria Escriva puts it, "Don't neglect your spiritual reading. Reading has made many saints."[9]

4. **Hear Daily Holy Mass and Receive Holy Communion:** This is the most important habit of all the seven. As such, it has to be at the very center of our interior life and consequently our day. St. Peter Julian Eymard tells us to "hear Mass daily; it will prosper the whole day. All your duties will be performed the better for it, and your soul will be stronger to bear its daily cross. The Mass is the most holy act of religion; you can do nothing that can give greater glory to God or be more profitable for your soul than to hear Mass both frequently and devoutly. It is the favorite devotion of the saints."

5. **Angelus (or Regina Coeli):** This is the very ancient Catholic custom that has us stop what we are doing to greet our Blessed Mother for a moment (at 6:00 a.m., 12:00 noon, and 6:00 p.m. daily), as any good child remembers his mother during the day, and to meditate on the Incarnation and Resurrection of our Lord, which give such meaning to our entire existence. The Regina Coeli is

said during the Easter season. The Angelus is said during the rest of the year.

6. Holy Rosary: As St. Josemaria Escriva puts it, "For those who use their intelligence and their study as a weapon, the Rosary is most effective, because this apparently monotonous way of beseeching Our Lady, as children do their mother, can destroy every seed of vainglory and pride."[10] Father McCloskey reminds us that "by repeating words of love to Mary and offering up each decade for our intentions, we take the shortcut to Jesus, which is to pass through the heart of Mary. He cannot refuse her anything!"[11] Pope Pius IX once said, "Give me an army saying the Rosary and I will conquer the world."

7. Nightly Examination of Conscience: Take a few minutes just before bed to review your day asking, "How have I behaved as a child of God?" It's also a great time to look at that "dominant fault" you need to improve upon in order to become a saint. Conclude these few minutes of reflection by praying three Hail Marys for purity and then pray the "Act of Contrition."

JOURNAL ONE: SEARCH AND RESCUE

This method only orders what we have been practicing together for centuries. It is hoped that this new order offers greater accessibility and spurs more to utilize the *Sancta Sanctis*! ("God's holy gifts for God's holy people!") and pray each other into heaven.

Here is the plan for our daily "special ops mission" of search and rescue:

Step One: Choose a saint and holy soul. First, choose a deceased loved one for whom you wish to pray into heaven. This can be a great nudge to get you to explore your family tree, but you are free to pray for a deceased loved one more than once. Now, choose a saint to pray with you for your deceased loved one. You might choose a saint that was your loved one's favorite saint, or you might pick the patron saint of fishing because your loved one liked to fish, or possibly the saint whose feast it is that day. Look on page 177 to see a listing of over 400 saints. There is a checkbox alongside each saint's name, which can be a great way for you to keep track of which saints you've recruited into your Holy Alliance. This devotion is a great opportunity to take the time to learn about each saint you are recruiting for your personal Holy Alliance. These days, that's as simple as a quick Internet search to read a paragraph or two about your new recruit.

Step Two: Pray with your saint for your holy soul in purgatory by choosing one of the "Big Four" (Rosary, stations, Scripture, or adoration) that allow for a plenary indulgence. Always ask your Guardian Angel to pray with you too. Be sure the conditions are present for receiving a plenary indulgence. If not, offer a partial indulgence that day for your holy soul in purgatory. (But always try your best to earn that one plenary indulgence offered each day.) Having offered an indulgence for a deceased loved one, that holy soul in purgatory now becomes a "grateful" holy soul who will now offer his/her prayers for you. The St. Gertrude prayer is a great way to conclude your prayers.

Step Three: "Never Leave A Fallen Comrade." After completing this indulgenced prayer, ask today's grateful holy soul, today's saint, and all those in your Holy Alliance to join you as you all pray together for a living loved one you believe needs to receive God's grace to grow in faith, hope, and love — who, in some ways, is caught in the clutches of worldliness. Pray the Chaplet of Divine Mercy. If the "fallen comrade" (living loved one) is a family member, add the "Prayer for Healing the Family Tree." You are free to pray for a fallen comrade (living loved one) more than once.

This method of search and rescue is what I like to call "Stealth Evangelization" because we, along with our Holy Alliance, are storming the gates of heaven to plead with God to pour out His grace on the fallen comrade (living loved one), and that comrade need not even know what we are up to.

Here is a secret weapon of which many are not aware. Jesus told St. Faustina, "When you say this prayer, with a contrite heart and with faith on behalf of some sinner, I will give him the grace of conversion."[12] This is the prayer:

"O Blood and Water, which gushed forth from the Heart of Jesus as a fount of Mercy for us, I trust in You."

You should pray this prayer at the beginning of your Chaplet of Divine Mercy for your fallen comrade. Also, don't be afraid to pray this "secret weapon prayer" repeatedly, in a stealthy way (inaudibly), for the fallen comrade while you may be seated near him or her. Pray with trust.

The following pages are a convenient journal for you to record your daily Search and Rescue Mission information.

In the weeks and months ahead, you will be able to look back at this journal and see the names of those who make up your growing Holy Alliance. Then you will certainly know that you are not alone!

How to use the Search and Rescue Journal:

1. Each day choose a deceased loved one (HOLY SOUL) to pray for and a saint (SAINT) to pray with. A list of over 400 saints is found starting on page 115. Write their names in the appropriate columns.

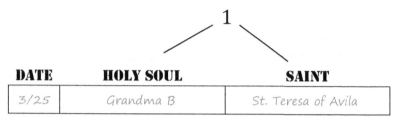

DATE	HOLY SOUL	SAINT
3/25	Grandma B	St. Teresa of Avila

2. Pray and put a check mark in the box next to one of the indulgenced prayers (OFFERING). Determine if the conditions are present for a plenary indulgence. If so, put a check mark next to "Plenary". If not, put a check mark next to "Partial."

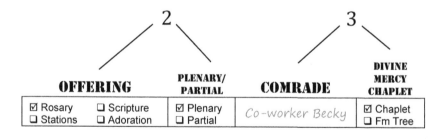

OFFERING		PLENARY/ PARTIAL	COMRADE	DIVINE MERCY CHAPLET
☑ Rosary ☐ Stations	☐ Scripture ☐ Adoration	☑ Plenary ☐ Partial	Co-worker Becky	☑ Chaplet ☐ Fm Tree

3. Write the name of a living soul (COMRADE) who is in need of a deepening of their faith, hope, and love. Pray the Divine Mercy Chaplet, and if he or she is a family member, conclude with the Prayer for Healing the Family Tree.

SEARCH AND RESCUE JOURNAL

SEARCH AND RESCUE

DATE	HOLY SOUL	SAINT

SEARCH AND RESCUE

OFFERING		PLENARY/ PARTIAL	COMRADE	DIVINE MERCY CHAPLET
❑ Rosary ❑ Stations	❑ Scripture ❑ Adoration	❑ Plenary ❑ Partial		❑ Chaplet ❑ Fm Tree
❑ Rosary ❑ Stations	❑ Scripture ❑ Adoration	❑ Plenary ❑ Partial		❑ Chaplet ❑ Fm Tree
❑ Rosary ❑ Stations	❑ Scripture ❑ Adoration	❑ Plenary ❑ Partial		❑ Chaplet ❑ Fm Tree
❑ Rosary ❑ Stations	❑ Scripture ❑ Adoration	❑ Plenary ❑ Partial		❑ Chaplet ❑ Fm Tree
❑ Rosary ❑ Stations	❑ Scripture ❑ Adoration	❑ Plenary ❑ Partial		❑ Chaplet ❑ Fm Tree
❑ Rosary ❑ Stations	❑ Scripture ❑ Adoration	❑ Plenary ❑ Partial		❑ Chaplet ❑ Fm Tree
❑ Rosary ❑ Stations	❑ Scripture ❑ Adoration	❑ Plenary ❑ Partial		❑ Chaplet ❑ Fm Tree
❑ Rosary ❑ Stations	❑ Scripture ❑ Adoration	❑ Plenary ❑ Partial		❑ Chaplet ❑ Fm Tree
❑ Rosary ❑ Stations	❑ Scripture ❑ Adoration	❑ Plenary ❑ Partial		❑ Chaplet ❑ Fm Tree
❑ Rosary ❑ Stations	❑ Scripture ❑ Adoration	❑ Plenary ❑ Partial		❑ Chaplet ❑ Fm Tree
❑ Rosary ❑ Stations	❑ Scripture ❑ Adoration	❑ Plenary ❑ Partial		❑ Chaplet ❑ Fm Tree
❑ Rosary ❑ Stations	❑ Scripture ❑ Adoration	❑ Plenary ❑ Partial		❑ Chaplet ❑ Fm Tree
❑ Rosary ❑ Stations	❑ Scripture ❑ Adoration	❑ Plenary ❑ Partial		❑ Chaplet ❑ Fm Tree
❑ Rosary ❑ Stations	❑ Scripture ❑ Adoration	❑ Plenary ❑ Partial		❑ Chaplet ❑ Fm Tree
❑ Rosary ❑ Stations	❑ Scripture ❑ Adoration	❑ Plenary ❑ Partial		❑ Chaplet ❑ Fm Tree
❑ Rosary ❑ Stations	❑ Scripture ❑ Adoration	❑ Plenary ❑ Partial		❑ Chaplet ❑ Fm Tree
❑ Rosary ❑ Stations	❑ Scripture ❑ Adoration	❑ Plenary ❑ Partial		❑ Chaplet ❑ Fm Tree
❑ Rosary ❑ Stations	❑ Scripture ❑ Adoration	❑ Plenary ❑ Partial		❑ Chaplet ❑ Fm Tree
❑ Rosary ❑ Stations	❑ Scripture ❑ Adoration	❑ Plenary ❑ Partial		❑ Chaplet ❑ Fm Tree
❑ Rosary ❑ Stations	❑ Scripture ❑ Adoration	❑ Plenary ❑ Partial		❑ Chaplet ❑ Fm Tree
❑ Rosary ❑ Stations	❑ Scripture ❑ Adoration	❑ Plenary ❑ Partial		❑ Chaplet ❑ Fm Tree

SEARCH AND RESCUE

DATE	HOLY SOUL	SAINT

SEARCH AND RESCUE

OFFERING		PLENARY/ PARTIAL	COMRADE	DIVINE MERCY CHAPLET
❏ Rosary ❏ Stations	❏ Scripture ❏ Adoration	❏ Plenary ❏ Partial		❏ Chaplet ❏ Fm Tree
❏ Rosary ❏ Stations	❏ Scripture ❏ Adoration	❏ Plenary ❏ Partial		❏ Chaplet ❏ Fm Tree
❏ Rosary ❏ Stations	❏ Scripture ❏ Adoration	❏ Plenary ❏ Partial		❏ Chaplet ❏ Fm Tree
❏ Rosary ❏ Stations	❏ Scripture ❏ Adoration	❏ Plenary ❏ Partial		❏ Chaplet ❏ Fm Tree
❏ Rosary ❏ Stations	❏ Scripture ❏ Adoration	❏ Plenary ❏ Partial		❏ Chaplet ❏ Fm Tree
❏ Rosary ❏ Stations	❏ Scripture ❏ Adoration	❏ Plenary ❏ Partial		❏ Chaplet ❏ Fm Tree
❏ Rosary ❏ Stations	❏ Scripture ❏ Adoration	❏ Plenary ❏ Partial		❏ Chaplet ❏ Fm Tree
❏ Rosary ❏ Stations	❏ Scripture ❏ Adoration	❏ Plenary ❏ Partial		❏ Chaplet ❏ Fm Tree
❏ Rosary ❏ Stations	❏ Scripture ❏ Adoration	❏ Plenary ❏ Partial		❏ Chaplet ❏ Fm Tree
❏ Rosary ❏ Stations	❏ Scripture ❏ Adoration	❏ Plenary ❏ Partial		❏ Chaplet ❏ Fm Tree
❏ Rosary ❏ Stations	❏ Scripture ❏ Adoration	❏ Plenary ❏ Partial		❏ Chaplet ❏ Fm Tree
❏ Rosary ❏ Stations	❏ Scripture ❏ Adoration	❏ Plenary ❏ Partial		❏ Chaplet ❏ Fm Tree
❏ Rosary ❏ Stations	❏ Scripture ❏ Adoration	❏ Plenary ❏ Partial		❏ Chaplet ❏ Fm Tree
❏ Rosary ❏ Stations	❏ Scripture ❏ Adoration	❏ Plenary ❏ Partial		❏ Chaplet ❏ Fm Tree
❏ Rosary ❏ Stations	❏ Scripture ❏ Adoration	❏ Plenary ❏ Partial		❏ Chaplet ❏ Fm Tree
❏ Rosary ❏ Stations	❏ Scripture ❏ Adoration	❏ Plenary ❏ Partial		❏ Chaplet ❏ Fm Tree
❏ Rosary ❏ Stations	❏ Scripture ❏ Adoration	❏ Plenary ❏ Partial		❏ Chaplet ❏ Fm Tree
❏ Rosary ❏ Stations	❏ Scripture ❏ Adoration	❏ Plenary ❏ Partial		❏ Chaplet ❏ Fm Tree
❏ Rosary ❏ Stations	❏ Scripture ❏ Adoration	❏ Plenary ❏ Partial		❏ Chaplet ❏ Fm Tree
❏ Rosary ❏ Stations	❏ Scripture ❏ Adoration	❏ Plenary ❏ Partial		❏ Chaplet ❏ Fm Tree
❏ Rosary ❏ Stations	❏ Scripture ❏ Adoration	❏ Plenary ❏ Partial		❏ Chaplet ❏ Fm Tree

SEARCH AND RESCUE

DATE	HOLY SOUL	SAINT

SEARCH AND RESCUE

OFFERING		PLENARY/ PARTIAL	COMRADE	DIVINE MERCY CHAPLET
❑ Rosary ❑ Stations	❑ Scripture ❑ Adoration	❑ Plenary ❑ Partial		❑ Chaplet ❑ Fm Tree
❑ Rosary ❑ Stations	❑ Scripture ❑ Adoration	❑ Plenary ❑ Partial		❑ Chaplet ❑ Fm Tree
❑ Rosary ❑ Stations	❑ Scripture ❑ Adoration	❑ Plenary ❑ Partial		❑ Chaplet ❑ Fm Tree
❑ Rosary ❑ Stations	❑ Scripture ❑ Adoration	❑ Plenary ❑ Partial		❑ Chaplet ❑ Fm Tree
❑ Rosary ❑ Stations	❑ Scripture ❑ Adoration	❑ Plenary ❑ Partial		❑ Chaplet ❑ Fm Tree
❑ Rosary ❑ Stations	❑ Scripture ❑ Adoration	❑ Plenary ❑ Partial		❑ Chaplet ❑ Fm Tree
❑ Rosary ❑ Stations	❑ Scripture ❑ Adoration	❑ Plenary ❑ Partial		❑ Chaplet ❑ Fm Tree
❑ Rosary ❑ Stations	❑ Scripture ❑ Adoration	❑ Plenary ❑ Partial		❑ Chaplet ❑ Fm Tree
❑ Rosary ❑ Stations	❑ Scripture ❑ Adoration	❑ Plenary ❑ Partial		❑ Chaplet ❑ Fm Tree
❑ Rosary ❑ Stations	❑ Scripture ❑ Adoration	❑ Plenary ❑ Partial		❑ Chaplet ❑ Fm Tree
❑ Rosary ❑ Stations	❑ Scripture ❑ Adoration	❑ Plenary ❑ Partial		❑ Chaplet ❑ Fm Tree
❑ Rosary ❑ Stations	❑ Scripture ❑ Adoration	❑ Plenary ❑ Partial		❑ Chaplet ❑ Fm Tree
❑ Rosary ❑ Stations	❑ Scripture ❑ Adoration	❑ Plenary ❑ Partial		❑ Chaplet ❑ Fm Tree
❑ Rosary ❑ Stations	❑ Scripture ❑ Adoration	❑ Plenary ❑ Partial		❑ Chaplet ❑ Fm Tree
❑ Rosary ❑ Stations	❑ Scripture ❑ Adoration	❑ Plenary ❑ Partial		❑ Chaplet ❑ Fm Tree
❑ Rosary ❑ Stations	❑ Scripture ❑ Adoration	❑ Plenary ❑ Partial		❑ Chaplet ❑ Fm Tree
❑ Rosary ❑ Stations	❑ Scripture ❑ Adoration	❑ Plenary ❑ Partial		❑ Chaplet ❑ Fm Tree
❑ Rosary ❑ Stations	❑ Scripture ❑ Adoration	❑ Plenary ❑ Partial		❑ Chaplet ❑ Fm Tree
❑ Rosary ❑ Stations	❑ Scripture ❑ Adoration	❑ Plenary ❑ Partial		❑ Chaplet ❑ Fm Tree
❑ Rosary ❑ Stations	❑ Scripture ❑ Adoration	❑ Plenary ❑ Partial		❑ Chaplet ❑ Fm Tree
❑ Rosary ❑ Stations	❑ Scripture ❑ Adoration	❑ Plenary ❑ Partial		❑ Chaplet ❑ Fm Tree

SEARCH AND RESCUE

DATE	HOLY SOUL	SAINT

SEARCH AND RESCUE

OFFERING		PLENARY/ PARTIAL	COMRADE	DIVINE MERCY CHAPLET
❏ Rosary ❏ Stations	❏ Scripture ❏ Adoration	❏ Plenary ❏ Partial		❏ Chaplet ❏ Fm Tree
❏ Rosary ❏ Stations	❏ Scripture ❏ Adoration	❏ Plenary ❏ Partial		❏ Chaplet ❏ Fm Tree
❏ Rosary ❏ Stations	❏ Scripture ❏ Adoration	❏ Plenary ❏ Partial		❏ Chaplet ❏ Fm Tree
❏ Rosary ❏ Stations	❏ Scripture ❏ Adoration	❏ Plenary ❏ Partial		❏ Chaplet ❏ Fm Tree
❏ Rosary ❏ Stations	❏ Scripture ❏ Adoration	❏ Plenary ❏ Partial		❏ Chaplet ❏ Fm Tree
❏ Rosary ❏ Stations	❏ Scripture ❏ Adoration	❏ Plenary ❏ Partial		❏ Chaplet ❏ Fm Tree
❏ Rosary ❏ Stations	❏ Scripture ❏ Adoration	❏ Plenary ❏ Partial		❏ Chaplet ❏ Fm Tree
❏ Rosary ❏ Stations	❏ Scripture ❏ Adoration	❏ Plenary ❏ Partial		❏ Chaplet ❏ Fm Tree
❏ Rosary ❏ Stations	❏ Scripture ❏ Adoration	❏ Plenary ❏ Partial		❏ Chaplet ❏ Fm Tree
❏ Rosary ❏ Stations	❏ Scripture ❏ Adoration	❏ Plenary ❏ Partial		❏ Chaplet ❏ Fm Tree
❏ Rosary ❏ Stations	❏ Scripture ❏ Adoration	❏ Plenary ❏ Partial		❏ Chaplet ❏ Fm Tree
❏ Rosary ❏ Stations	❏ Scripture ❏ Adoration	❏ Plenary ❏ Partial		❏ Chaplet ❏ Fm Tree
❏ Rosary ❏ Stations	❏ Scripture ❏ Adoration	❏ Plenary ❏ Partial		❏ Chaplet ❏ Fm Tree
❏ Rosary ❏ Stations	❏ Scripture ❏ Adoration	❏ Plenary ❏ Partial		❏ Chaplet ❏ Fm Tree
❏ Rosary ❏ Stations	❏ Scripture ❏ Adoration	❏ Plenary ❏ Partial		❏ Chaplet ❏ Fm Tree
❏ Rosary ❏ Stations	❏ Scripture ❏ Adoration	❏ Plenary ❏ Partial		❏ Chaplet ❏ Fm Tree
❏ Rosary ❏ Stations	❏ Scripture ❏ Adoration	❏ Plenary ❏ Partial		❏ Chaplet ❏ Fm Tree
❏ Rosary ❏ Stations	❏ Scripture ❏ Adoration	❏ Plenary ❏ Partial		❏ Chaplet ❏ Fm Tree
❏ Rosary ❏ Stations	❏ Scripture ❏ Adoration	❏ Plenary ❏ Partial		❏ Chaplet ❏ Fm Tree
❏ Rosary ❏ Stations	❏ Scripture ❏ Adoration	❏ Plenary ❏ Partial		❏ Chaplet ❏ Fm Tree
❏ Rosary ❏ Stations	❏ Scripture ❏ Adoration	❏ Plenary ❏ Partial		❏ Chaplet ❏ Fm Tree

SEARCH AND RESCUE

DATE	HOLY SOUL	SAINT

SEARCH AND RESCUE

OFFERING		PLENARY/ PARTIAL	COMRADE	DIVINE MERCY CHAPLET
❑ Rosary ❑ Stations	❑ Scripture ❑ Adoration	❑ Plenary ❑ Partial		❑ Chaplet ❑ Fm Tree
❑ Rosary ❑ Stations	❑ Scripture ❑ Adoration	❑ Plenary ❑ Partial		❑ Chaplet ❑ Fm Tree
❑ Rosary ❑ Stations	❑ Scripture ❑ Adoration	❑ Plenary ❑ Partial		❑ Chaplet ❑ Fm Tree
❑ Rosary ❑ Stations	❑ Scripture ❑ Adoration	❑ Plenary ❑ Partial		❑ Chaplet ❑ Fm Tree
❑ Rosary ❑ Stations	❑ Scripture ❑ Adoration	❑ Plenary ❑ Partial		❑ Chaplet ❑ Fm Tree
❑ Rosary ❑ Stations	❑ Scripture ❑ Adoration	❑ Plenary ❑ Partial		❑ Chaplet ❑ Fm Tree
❑ Rosary ❑ Stations	❑ Scripture ❑ Adoration	❑ Plenary ❑ Partial		❑ Chaplet ❑ Fm Tree
❑ Rosary ❑ Stations	❑ Scripture ❑ Adoration	❑ Plenary ❑ Partial		❑ Chaplet ❑ Fm Tree
❑ Rosary ❑ Stations	❑ Scripture ❑ Adoration	❑ Plenary ❑ Partial		❑ Chaplet ❑ Fm Tree
❑ Rosary ❑ Stations	❑ Scripture ❑ Adoration	❑ Plenary ❑ Partial		❑ Chaplet ❑ Fm Tree
❑ Rosary ❑ Stations	❑ Scripture ❑ Adoration	❑ Plenary ❑ Partial		❑ Chaplet ❑ Fm Tree
❑ Rosary ❑ Stations	❑ Scripture ❑ Adoration	❑ Plenary ❑ Partial		❑ Chaplet ❑ Fm Tree
❑ Rosary ❑ Stations	❑ Scripture ❑ Adoration	❑ Plenary ❑ Partial		❑ Chaplet ❑ Fm Tree
❑ Rosary ❑ Stations	❑ Scripture ❑ Adoration	❑ Plenary ❑ Partial		❑ Chaplet ❑ Fm Tree
❑ Rosary ❑ Stations	❑ Scripture ❑ Adoration	❑ Plenary ❑ Partial		❑ Chaplet ❑ Fm Tree
❑ Rosary ❑ Stations	❑ Scripture ❑ Adoration	❑ Plenary ❑ Partial		❑ Chaplet ❑ Fm Tree
❑ Rosary ❑ Stations	❑ Scripture ❑ Adoration	❑ Plenary ❑ Partial		❑ Chaplet ❑ Fm Tree
❑ Rosary ❑ Stations	❑ Scripture ❑ Adoration	❑ Plenary ❑ Partial		❑ Chaplet ❑ Fm Tree
❑ Rosary ❑ Stations	❑ Scripture ❑ Adoration	❑ Plenary ❑ Partial		❑ Chaplet ❑ Fm Tree
❑ Rosary ❑ Stations	❑ Scripture ❑ Adoration	❑ Plenary ❑ Partial		❑ Chaplet ❑ Fm Tree

SEARCH AND RESCUE

DATE	HOLY SOUL	SAINT

SEARCH AND RESCUE

OFFERING		PLENARY/ PARTIAL	COMRADE	DIVINE MERCY CHAPLET
❑ Rosary ❑ Stations	❑ Scripture ❑ Adoration	❑ Plenary ❑ Partial		❑ Chaplet ❑ Fm Tree
❑ Rosary ❑ Stations	❑ Scripture ❑ Adoration	❑ Plenary ❑ Partial		❑ Chaplet ❑ Fm Tree
❑ Rosary ❑ Stations	❑ Scripture ❑ Adoration	❑ Plenary ❑ Partial		❑ Chaplet ❑ Fm Tree
❑ Rosary ❑ Stations	❑ Scripture ❑ Adoration	❑ Plenary ❑ Partial		❑ Chaplet ❑ Fm Tree
❑ Rosary ❑ Stations	❑ Scripture ❑ Adoration	❑ Plenary ❑ Partial		❑ Chaplet ❑ Fm Tree
❑ Rosary ❑ Stations	❑ Scripture ❑ Adoration	❑ Plenary ❑ Partial		❑ Chaplet ❑ Fm Tree
❑ Rosary ❑ Stations	❑ Scripture ❑ Adoration	❑ Plenary ❑ Partial		❑ Chaplet ❑ Fm Tree
❑ Rosary ❑ Stations	❑ Scripture ❑ Adoration	❑ Plenary ❑ Partial		❑ Chaplet ❑ Fm Tree
❑ Rosary ❑ Stations	❑ Scripture ❑ Adoration	❑ Plenary ❑ Partial		❑ Chaplet ❑ Fm Tree
❑ Rosary ❑ Stations	❑ Scripture ❑ Adoration	❑ Plenary ❑ Partial		❑ Chaplet ❑ Fm Tree
❑ Rosary ❑ Stations	❑ Scripture ❑ Adoration	❑ Plenary ❑ Partial		❑ Chaplet ❑ Fm Tree
❑ Rosary ❑ Stations	❑ Scripture ❑ Adoration	❑ Plenary ❑ Partial		❑ Chaplet ❑ Fm Tree
❑ Rosary ❑ Stations	❑ Scripture ❑ Adoration	❑ Plenary ❑ Partial		❑ Chaplet ❑ Fm Tree
❑ Rosary ❑ Stations	❑ Scripture ❑ Adoration	❑ Plenary ❑ Partial		❑ Chaplet ❑ Fm Tree
❑ Rosary ❑ Stations	❑ Scripture ❑ Adoration	❑ Plenary ❑ Partial		❑ Chaplet ❑ Fm Tree
❑ Rosary ❑ Stations	❑ Scripture ❑ Adoration	❑ Plenary ❑ Partial		❑ Chaplet ❑ Fm Tree
❑ Rosary ❑ Stations	❑ Scripture ❑ Adoration	❑ Plenary ❑ Partial		❑ Chaplet ❑ Fm Tree
❑ Rosary ❑ Stations	❑ Scripture ❑ Adoration	❑ Plenary ❑ Partial		❑ Chaplet ❑ Fm Tree
❑ Rosary ❑ Stations	❑ Scripture ❑ Adoration	❑ Plenary ❑ Partial		❑ Chaplet ❑ Fm Tree
❑ Rosary ❑ Stations	❑ Scripture ❑ Adoration	❑ Plenary ❑ Partial		❑ Chaplet ❑ Fm Tree
❑ Rosary ❑ Stations	❑ Scripture ❑ Adoration	❑ Plenary ❑ Partial		❑ Chaplet ❑ Fm Tree

SEARCH AND RESCUE

DATE	HOLY SOUL	SAINT

SEARCH AND RESCUE

OFFERING		PLENARY/ PARTIAL	COMRADE	DIVINE MERCY CHAPLET
❏ Rosary ❏ Stations	❏ Scripture ❏ Adoration	❏ Plenary ❏ Partial		❏ Chaplet ❏ Fm Tree
❏ Rosary ❏ Stations	❏ Scripture ❏ Adoration	❏ Plenary ❏ Partial		❏ Chaplet ❏ Fm Tree
❏ Rosary ❏ Stations	❏ Scripture ❏ Adoration	❏ Plenary ❏ Partial		❏ Chaplet ❏ Fm Tree
❏ Rosary ❏ Stations	❏ Scripture ❏ Adoration	❏ Plenary ❏ Partial		❏ Chaplet ❏ Fm Tree
❏ Rosary ❏ Stations	❏ Scripture ❏ Adoration	❏ Plenary ❏ Partial		❏ Chaplet ❏ Fm Tree
❏ Rosary ❏ Stations	❏ Scripture ❏ Adoration	❏ Plenary ❏ Partial		❏ Chaplet ❏ Fm Tree
❏ Rosary ❏ Stations	❏ Scripture ❏ Adoration	❏ Plenary ❏ Partial		❏ Chaplet ❏ Fm Tree
❏ Rosary ❏ Stations	❏ Scripture ❏ Adoration	❏ Plenary ❏ Partial		❏ Chaplet ❏ Fm Tree
❏ Rosary ❏ Stations	❏ Scripture ❏ Adoration	❏ Plenary ❏ Partial		❏ Chaplet ❏ Fm Tree
❏ Rosary ❏ Stations	❏ Scripture ❏ Adoration	❏ Plenary ❏ Partial		❏ Chaplet ❏ Fm Tree
❏ Rosary ❏ Stations	❏ Scripture ❏ Adoration	❏ Plenary ❏ Partial		❏ Chaplet ❏ Fm Tree
❏ Rosary ❏ Stations	❏ Scripture ❏ Adoration	❏ Plenary ❏ Partial		❏ Chaplet ❏ Fm Tree
❏ Rosary ❏ Stations	❏ Scripture ❏ Adoration	❏ Plenary ❏ Partial		❏ Chaplet ❏ Fm Tree
❏ Rosary ❏ Stations	❏ Scripture ❏ Adoration	❏ Plenary ❏ Partial		❏ Chaplet ❏ Fm Tree
❏ Rosary ❏ Stations	❏ Scripture ❏ Adoration	❏ Plenary ❏ Partial		❏ Chaplet ❏ Fm Tree
❏ Rosary ❏ Stations	❏ Scripture ❏ Adoration	❏ Plenary ❏ Partial		❏ Chaplet ❏ Fm Tree
❏ Rosary ❏ Stations	❏ Scripture ❏ Adoration	❏ Plenary ❏ Partial		❏ Chaplet ❏ Fm Tree
❏ Rosary ❏ Stations	❏ Scripture ❏ Adoration	❏ Plenary ❏ Partial		❏ Chaplet ❏ Fm Tree
❏ Rosary ❏ Stations	❏ Scripture ❏ Adoration	❏ Plenary ❏ Partial		❏ Chaplet ❏ Fm Tree
❏ Rosary ❏ Stations	❏ Scripture ❏ Adoration	❏ Plenary ❏ Partial		❏ Chaplet ❏ Fm Tree
❏ Rosary ❏ Stations	❏ Scripture ❏ Adoration	❏ Plenary ❏ Partial		❏ Chaplet ❏ Fm Tree

SEARCH AND RESCUE

DATE	HOLY SOUL	SAINT

SEARCH AND RESCUE

OFFERING		PLENARY/ PARTIAL	COMRADE	DIVINE MERCY CHAPLET
❏ Rosary ❏ Stations	❏ Scripture ❏ Adoration	❏ Plenary ❏ Partial		❏ Chaplet ❏ Fm Tree
❏ Rosary ❏ Stations	❏ Scripture ❏ Adoration	❏ Plenary ❏ Partial		❏ Chaplet ❏ Fm Tree
❏ Rosary ❏ Stations	❏ Scripture ❏ Adoration	❏ Plenary ❏ Partial		❏ Chaplet ❏ Fm Tree
❏ Rosary ❏ Stations	❏ Scripture ❏ Adoration	❏ Plenary ❏ Partial		❏ Chaplet ❏ Fm Tree
❏ Rosary ❏ Stations	❏ Scripture ❏ Adoration	❏ Plenary ❏ Partial		❏ Chaplet ❏ Fm Tree
❏ Rosary ❏ Stations	❏ Scripture ❏ Adoration	❏ Plenary ❏ Partial		❏ Chaplet ❏ Fm Tree
❏ Rosary ❏ Stations	❏ Scripture ❏ Adoration	❏ Plenary ❏ Partial		❏ Chaplet ❏ Fm Tree
❏ Rosary ❏ Stations	❏ Scripture ❏ Adoration	❏ Plenary ❏ Partial		❏ Chaplet ❏ Fm Tree
❏ Rosary ❏ Stations	❏ Scripture ❏ Adoration	❏ Plenary ❏ Partial		❏ Chaplet ❏ Fm Tree
❏ Rosary ❏ Stations	❏ Scripture ❏ Adoration	❏ Plenary ❏ Partial		❏ Chaplet ❏ Fm Tree
❏ Rosary ❏ Stations	❏ Scripture ❏ Adoration	❏ Plenary ❏ Partial		❏ Chaplet ❏ Fm Tree
❏ Rosary ❏ Stations	❏ Scripture ❏ Adoration	❏ Plenary ❏ Partial		❏ Chaplet ❏ Fm Tree
❏ Rosary ❏ Stations	❏ Scripture ❏ Adoration	❏ Plenary ❏ Partial		❏ Chaplet ❏ Fm Tree
❏ Rosary ❏ Stations	❏ Scripture ❏ Adoration	❏ Plenary ❏ Partial		❏ Chaplet ❏ Fm Tree
❏ Rosary ❏ Stations	❏ Scripture ❏ Adoration	❏ Plenary ❏ Partial		❏ Chaplet ❏ Fm Tree
❏ Rosary ❏ Stations	❏ Scripture ❏ Adoration	❏ Plenary ❏ Partial		❏ Chaplet ❏ Fm Tree
❏ Rosary ❏ Stations	❏ Scripture ❏ Adoration	❏ Plenary ❏ Partial		❏ Chaplet ❏ Fm Tree
❏ Rosary ❏ Stations	❏ Scripture ❏ Adoration	❏ Plenary ❏ Partial		❏ Chaplet ❏ Fm Tree
❏ Rosary ❏ Stations	❏ Scripture ❏ Adoration	❏ Plenary ❏ Partial		❏ Chaplet ❏ Fm Tree
❏ Rosary ❏ Stations	❏ Scripture ❏ Adoration	❏ Plenary ❏ Partial		❏ Chaplet ❏ Fm Tree
❏ Rosary ❏ Stations	❏ Scripture ❏ Adoration	❏ Plenary ❏ Partial		❏ Chaplet ❏ Fm Tree

SEARCH AND RESCUE

DATE	HOLY SOUL	SAINT

SEARCH AND RESCUE

OFFERING		PLENARY/ PARTIAL	COMRADE	DIVINE MERCY CHAPLET
❑ Rosary ❑ Stations	❑ Scripture ❑ Adoration	❑ Plenary ❑ Partial		❑ Chaplet ❑ Fm Tree
❑ Rosary ❑ Stations	❑ Scripture ❑ Adoration	❑ Plenary ❑ Partial		❑ Chaplet ❑ Fm Tree
❑ Rosary ❑ Stations	❑ Scripture ❑ Adoration	❑ Plenary ❑ Partial		❑ Chaplet ❑ Fm Tree
❑ Rosary ❑ Stations	❑ Scripture ❑ Adoration	❑ Plenary ❑ Partial		❑ Chaplet ❑ Fm Tree
❑ Rosary ❑ Stations	❑ Scripture ❑ Adoration	❑ Plenary ❑ Partial		❑ Chaplet ❑ Fm Tree
❑ Rosary ❑ Stations	❑ Scripture ❑ Adoration	❑ Plenary ❑ Partial		❑ Chaplet ❑ Fm Tree
❑ Rosary ❑ Stations	❑ Scripture ❑ Adoration	❑ Plenary ❑ Partial		❑ Chaplet ❑ Fm Tree
❑ Rosary ❑ Stations	❑ Scripture ❑ Adoration	❑ Plenary ❑ Partial		❑ Chaplet ❑ Fm Tree
❑ Rosary ❑ Stations	❑ Scripture ❑ Adoration	❑ Plenary ❑ Partial		❑ Chaplet ❑ Fm Tree
❑ Rosary ❑ Stations	❑ Scripture ❑ Adoration	❑ Plenary ❑ Partial		❑ Chaplet ❑ Fm Tree
❑ Rosary ❑ Stations	❑ Scripture ❑ Adoration	❑ Plenary ❑ Partial		❑ Chaplet ❑ Fm Tree
❑ Rosary ❑ Stations	❑ Scripture ❑ Adoration	❑ Plenary ❑ Partial		❑ Chaplet ❑ Fm Tree
❑ Rosary ❑ Stations	❑ Scripture ❑ Adoration	❑ Plenary ❑ Partial		❑ Chaplet ❑ Fm Tree
❑ Rosary ❑ Stations	❑ Scripture ❑ Adoration	❑ Plenary ❑ Partial		❑ Chaplet ❑ Fm Tree
❑ Rosary ❑ Stations	❑ Scripture ❑ Adoration	❑ Plenary ❑ Partial		❑ Chaplet ❑ Fm Tree
❑ Rosary ❑ Stations	❑ Scripture ❑ Adoration	❑ Plenary ❑ Partial		❑ Chaplet ❑ Fm Tree
❑ Rosary ❑ Stations	❑ Scripture ❑ Adoration	❑ Plenary ❑ Partial		❑ Chaplet ❑ Fm Tree
❑ Rosary ❑ Stations	❑ Scripture ❑ Adoration	❑ Plenary ❑ Partial		❑ Chaplet ❑ Fm Tree
❑ Rosary ❑ Stations	❑ Scripture ❑ Adoration	❑ Plenary ❑ Partial		❑ Chaplet ❑ Fm Tree
❑ Rosary ❑ Stations	❑ Scripture ❑ Adoration	❑ Plenary ❑ Partial		❑ Chaplet ❑ Fm Tree

SEARCH AND RESCUE

DATE	HOLY SOUL	SAINT

SEARCH AND RESCUE

OFFERING		PLENARY/ PARTIAL	COMRADE	DIVINE MERCY CHAPLET
❑ Rosary ❑ Stations	❑ Scripture ❑ Adoration	❑ Plenary ❑ Partial		❑ Chaplet ❑ Fm Tree
❑ Rosary ❑ Stations	❑ Scripture ❑ Adoration	❑ Plenary ❑ Partial		❑ Chaplet ❑ Fm Tree
❑ Rosary ❑ Stations	❑ Scripture ❑ Adoration	❑ Plenary ❑ Partial		❑ Chaplet ❑ Fm Tree
❑ Rosary ❑ Stations	❑ Scripture ❑ Adoration	❑ Plenary ❑ Partial		❑ Chaplet ❑ Fm Tree
❑ Rosary ❑ Stations	❑ Scripture ❑ Adoration	❑ Plenary ❑ Partial		❑ Chaplet ❑ Fm Tree
❑ Rosary ❑ Stations	❑ Scripture ❑ Adoration	❑ Plenary ❑ Partial		❑ Chaplet ❑ Fm Tree
❑ Rosary ❑ Stations	❑ Scripture ❑ Adoration	❑ Plenary ❑ Partial		❑ Chaplet ❑ Fm Tree
❑ Rosary ❑ Stations	❑ Scripture ❑ Adoration	❑ Plenary ❑ Partial		❑ Chaplet ❑ Fm Tree
❑ Rosary ❑ Stations	❑ Scripture ❑ Adoration	❑ Plenary ❑ Partial		❑ Chaplet ❑ Fm Tree
❑ Rosary ❑ Stations	❑ Scripture ❑ Adoration	❑ Plenary ❑ Partial		❑ Chaplet ❑ Fm Tree
❑ Rosary ❑ Stations	❑ Scripture ❑ Adoration	❑ Plenary ❑ Partial		❑ Chaplet ❑ Fm Tree
❑ Rosary ❑ Stations	❑ Scripture ❑ Adoration	❑ Plenary ❑ Partial		❑ Chaplet ❑ Fm Tree
❑ Rosary ❑ Stations	❑ Scripture ❑ Adoration	❑ Plenary ❑ Partial		❑ Chaplet ❑ Fm Tree
❑ Rosary ❑ Stations	❑ Scripture ❑ Adoration	❑ Plenary ❑ Partial		❑ Chaplet ❑ Fm Tree
❑ Rosary ❑ Stations	❑ Scripture ❑ Adoration	❑ Plenary ❑ Partial		❑ Chaplet ❑ Fm Tree
❑ Rosary ❑ Stations	❑ Scripture ❑ Adoration	❑ Plenary ❑ Partial		❑ Chaplet ❑ Fm Tree
❑ Rosary ❑ Stations	❑ Scripture ❑ Adoration	❑ Plenary ❑ Partial		❑ Chaplet ❑ Fm Tree
❑ Rosary ❑ Stations	❑ Scripture ❑ Adoration	❑ Plenary ❑ Partial		❑ Chaplet ❑ Fm Tree
❑ Rosary ❑ Stations	❑ Scripture ❑ Adoration	❑ Plenary ❑ Partial		❑ Chaplet ❑ Fm Tree
❑ Rosary ❑ Stations	❑ Scripture ❑ Adoration	❑ Plenary ❑ Partial		❑ Chaplet ❑ Fm Tree
❑ Rosary ❑ Stations	❑ Scripture ❑ Adoration	❑ Plenary ❑ Partial		❑ Chaplet ❑ Fm Tree

SEARCH AND RESCUE

DATE	HOLY SOUL	SAINT

SEARCH AND RESCUE

OFFERING		PLENARY/ PARTIAL	COMRADE	DIVINE MERCY CHAPLET
❏ Rosary ❏ Stations	❏ Scripture ❏ Adoration	❏ Plenary ❏ Partial		❏ Chaplet ❏ Fm Tree
❏ Rosary ❏ Stations	❏ Scripture ❏ Adoration	❏ Plenary ❏ Partial		❏ Chaplet ❏ Fm Tree
❏ Rosary ❏ Stations	❏ Scripture ❏ Adoration	❏ Plenary ❏ Partial		❏ Chaplet ❏ Fm Tree
❏ Rosary ❏ Stations	❏ Scripture ❏ Adoration	❏ Plenary ❏ Partial		❏ Chaplet ❏ Fm Tree
❏ Rosary ❏ Stations	❏ Scripture ❏ Adoration	❏ Plenary ❏ Partial		❏ Chaplet ❏ Fm Tree
❏ Rosary ❏ Stations	❏ Scripture ❏ Adoration	❏ Plenary ❏ Partial		❏ Chaplet ❏ Fm Tree
❏ Rosary ❏ Stations	❏ Scripture ❏ Adoration	❏ Plenary ❏ Partial		❏ Chaplet ❏ Fm Tree
❏ Rosary ❏ Stations	❏ Scripture ❏ Adoration	❏ Plenary ❏ Partial		❏ Chaplet ❏ Fm Tree
❏ Rosary ❏ Stations	❏ Scripture ❏ Adoration	❏ Plenary ❏ Partial		❏ Chaplet ❏ Fm Tree
❏ Rosary ❏ Stations	❏ Scripture ❏ Adoration	❏ Plenary ❏ Partial		❏ Chaplet ❏ Fm Tree
❏ Rosary ❏ Stations	❏ Scripture ❏ Adoration	❏ Plenary ❏ Partial		❏ Chaplet ❏ Fm Tree
❏ Rosary ❏ Stations	❏ Scripture ❏ Adoration	❏ Plenary ❏ Partial		❏ Chaplet ❏ Fm Tree
❏ Rosary ❏ Stations	❏ Scripture ❏ Adoration	❏ Plenary ❏ Partial		❏ Chaplet ❏ Fm Tree
❏ Rosary ❏ Stations	❏ Scripture ❏ Adoration	❏ Plenary ❏ Partial		❏ Chaplet ❏ Fm Tree
❏ Rosary ❏ Stations	❏ Scripture ❏ Adoration	❏ Plenary ❏ Partial		❏ Chaplet ❏ Fm Tree
❏ Rosary ❏ Stations	❏ Scripture ❏ Adoration	❏ Plenary ❏ Partial		❏ Chaplet ❏ Fm Tree
❏ Rosary ❏ Stations	❏ Scripture ❏ Adoration	❏ Plenary ❏ Partial		❏ Chaplet ❏ Fm Tree
❏ Rosary ❏ Stations	❏ Scripture ❏ Adoration	❏ Plenary ❏ Partial		❏ Chaplet ❏ Fm Tree
❏ Rosary ❏ Stations	❏ Scripture ❏ Adoration	❏ Plenary ❏ Partial		❏ Chaplet ❏ Fm Tree
❏ Rosary ❏ Stations	❏ Scripture ❏ Adoration	❏ Plenary ❏ Partial		❏ Chaplet ❏ Fm Tree

SEARCH AND RESCUE

DATE	HOLY SOUL	SAINT

SEARCH AND RESCUE

OFFERING		PLENARY/ PARTIAL	COMRADE	DIVINE MERCY CHAPLET
❑ Rosary ❑ Stations	❑ Scripture ❑ Adoration	❑ Plenary ❑ Partial		❑ Chaplet ❑ Fm Tree
❑ Rosary ❑ Stations	❑ Scripture ❑ Adoration	❑ Plenary ❑ Partial		❑ Chaplet ❑ Fm Tree
❑ Rosary ❑ Stations	❑ Scripture ❑ Adoration	❑ Plenary ❑ Partial		❑ Chaplet ❑ Fm Tree
❑ Rosary ❑ Stations	❑ Scripture ❑ Adoration	❑ Plenary ❑ Partial		❑ Chaplet ❑ Fm Tree
❑ Rosary ❑ Stations	❑ Scripture ❑ Adoration	❑ Plenary ❑ Partial		❑ Chaplet ❑ Fm Tree
❑ Rosary ❑ Stations	❑ Scripture ❑ Adoration	❑ Plenary ❑ Partial		❑ Chaplet ❑ Fm Tree
❑ Rosary ❑ Stations	❑ Scripture ❑ Adoration	❑ Plenary ❑ Partial		❑ Chaplet ❑ Fm Tree
❑ Rosary ❑ Stations	❑ Scripture ❑ Adoration	❑ Plenary ❑ Partial		❑ Chaplet ❑ Fm Tree
❑ Rosary ❑ Stations	❑ Scripture ❑ Adoration	❑ Plenary ❑ Partial		❑ Chaplet ❑ Fm Tree
❑ Rosary ❑ Stations	❑ Scripture ❑ Adoration	❑ Plenary ❑ Partial		❑ Chaplet ❑ Fm Tree
❑ Rosary ❑ Stations	❑ Scripture ❑ Adoration	❑ Plenary ❑ Partial		❑ Chaplet ❑ Fm Tree
❑ Rosary ❑ Stations	❑ Scripture ❑ Adoration	❑ Plenary ❑ Partial		❑ Chaplet ❑ Fm Tree
❑ Rosary ❑ Stations	❑ Scripture ❑ Adoration	❑ Plenary ❑ Partial		❑ Chaplet ❑ Fm Tree
❑ Rosary ❑ Stations	❑ Scripture ❑ Adoration	❑ Plenary ❑ Partial		❑ Chaplet ❑ Fm Tree
❑ Rosary ❑ Stations	❑ Scripture ❑ Adoration	❑ Plenary ❑ Partial		❑ Chaplet ❑ Fm Tree
❑ Rosary ❑ Stations	❑ Scripture ❑ Adoration	❑ Plenary ❑ Partial		❑ Chaplet ❑ Fm Tree
❑ Rosary ❑ Stations	❑ Scripture ❑ Adoration	❑ Plenary ❑ Partial		❑ Chaplet ❑ Fm Tree
❑ Rosary ❑ Stations	❑ Scripture ❑ Adoration	❑ Plenary ❑ Partial		❑ Chaplet ❑ Fm Tree
❑ Rosary ❑ Stations	❑ Scripture ❑ Adoration	❑ Plenary ❑ Partial		❑ Chaplet ❑ Fm Tree
❑ Rosary ❑ Stations	❑ Scripture ❑ Adoration	❑ Plenary ❑ Partial		❑ Chaplet ❑ Fm Tree

SEARCH AND RESCUE

DATE	HOLY SOUL	SAINT

SEARCH AND RESCUE

OFFERING		PLENARY/ PARTIAL	COMRADE	DIVINE MERCY CHAPLET
❑ Rosary ❑ Stations	❑ Scripture ❑ Adoration	❑ Plenary ❑ Partial		❑ Chaplet ❑ Fm Tree
❑ Rosary ❑ Stations	❑ Scripture ❑ Adoration	❑ Plenary ❑ Partial		❑ Chaplet ❑ Fm Tree
❑ Rosary ❑ Stations	❑ Scripture ❑ Adoration	❑ Plenary ❑ Partial		❑ Chaplet ❑ Fm Tree
❑ Rosary ❑ Stations	❑ Scripture ❑ Adoration	❑ Plenary ❑ Partial		❑ Chaplet ❑ Fm Tree
❑ Rosary ❑ Stations	❑ Scripture ❑ Adoration	❑ Plenary ❑ Partial		❑ Chaplet ❑ Fm Tree
❑ Rosary ❑ Stations	❑ Scripture ❑ Adoration	❑ Plenary ❑ Partial		❑ Chaplet ❑ Fm Tree
❑ Rosary ❑ Stations	❑ Scripture ❑ Adoration	❑ Plenary ❑ Partial		❑ Chaplet ❑ Fm Tree
❑ Rosary ❑ Stations	❑ Scripture ❑ Adoration	❑ Plenary ❑ Partial		❑ Chaplet ❑ Fm Tree
❑ Rosary ❑ Stations	❑ Scripture ❑ Adoration	❑ Plenary ❑ Partial		❑ Chaplet ❑ Fm Tree
❑ Rosary ❑ Stations	❑ Scripture ❑ Adoration	❑ Plenary ❑ Partial		❑ Chaplet ❑ Fm Tree
❑ Rosary ❑ Stations	❑ Scripture ❑ Adoration	❑ Plenary ❑ Partial		❑ Chaplet ❑ Fm Tree
❑ Rosary ❑ Stations	❑ Scripture ❑ Adoration	❑ Plenary ❑ Partial		❑ Chaplet ❑ Fm Tree
❑ Rosary ❑ Stations	❑ Scripture ❑ Adoration	❑ Plenary ❑ Partial		❑ Chaplet ❑ Fm Tree
❑ Rosary ❑ Stations	❑ Scripture ❑ Adoration	❑ Plenary ❑ Partial		❑ Chaplet ❑ Fm Tree
❑ Rosary ❑ Stations	❑ Scripture ❑ Adoration	❑ Plenary ❑ Partial		❑ Chaplet ❑ Fm Tree
❑ Rosary ❑ Stations	❑ Scripture ❑ Adoration	❑ Plenary ❑ Partial		❑ Chaplet ❑ Fm Tree
❑ Rosary ❑ Stations	❑ Scripture ❑ Adoration	❑ Plenary ❑ Partial		❑ Chaplet ❑ Fm Tree
❑ Rosary ❑ Stations	❑ Scripture ❑ Adoration	❑ Plenary ❑ Partial		❑ Chaplet ❑ Fm Tree
❑ Rosary ❑ Stations	❑ Scripture ❑ Adoration	❑ Plenary ❑ Partial		❑ Chaplet ❑ Fm Tree
❑ Rosary ❑ Stations	❑ Scripture ❑ Adoration	❑ Plenary ❑ Partial		❑ Chaplet ❑ Fm Tree

SEARCH AND RESCUE

DATE	HOLY SOUL	SAINT

SEARCH AND RESCUE

OFFERING		PLENARY/ PARTIAL	COMRADE	DIVINE MERCY CHAPLET
❑ Rosary ❑ Stations	❑ Scripture ❑ Adoration	❑ Plenary ❑ Partial		❑ Chaplet ❑ Fm Tree
❑ Rosary ❑ Stations	❑ Scripture ❑ Adoration	❑ Plenary ❑ Partial		❑ Chaplet ❑ Fm Tree
❑ Rosary ❑ Stations	❑ Scripture ❑ Adoration	❑ Plenary ❑ Partial		❑ Chaplet ❑ Fm Tree
❑ Rosary ❑ Stations	❑ Scripture ❑ Adoration	❑ Plenary ❑ Partial		❑ Chaplet ❑ Fm Tree
❑ Rosary ❑ Stations	❑ Scripture ❑ Adoration	❑ Plenary ❑ Partial		❑ Chaplet ❑ Fm Tree
❑ Rosary ❑ Stations	❑ Scripture ❑ Adoration	❑ Plenary ❑ Partial		❑ Chaplet ❑ Fm Tree
❑ Rosary ❑ Stations	❑ Scripture ❑ Adoration	❑ Plenary ❑ Partial		❑ Chaplet ❑ Fm Tree
❑ Rosary ❑ Stations	❑ Scripture ❑ Adoration	❑ Plenary ❑ Partial		❑ Chaplet ❑ Fm Tree
❑ Rosary ❑ Stations	❑ Scripture ❑ Adoration	❑ Plenary ❑ Partial		❑ Chaplet ❑ Fm Tree
❑ Rosary ❑ Stations	❑ Scripture ❑ Adoration	❑ Plenary ❑ Partial		❑ Chaplet ❑ Fm Tree
❑ Rosary ❑ Stations	❑ Scripture ❑ Adoration	❑ Plenary ❑ Partial		❑ Chaplet ❑ Fm Tree
❑ Rosary ❑ Stations	❑ Scripture ❑ Adoration	❑ Plenary ❑ Partial		❑ Chaplet ❑ Fm Tree
❑ Rosary ❑ Stations	❑ Scripture ❑ Adoration	❑ Plenary ❑ Partial		❑ Chaplet ❑ Fm Tree
❑ Rosary ❑ Stations	❑ Scripture ❑ Adoration	❑ Plenary ❑ Partial		❑ Chaplet ❑ Fm Tree
❑ Rosary ❑ Stations	❑ Scripture ❑ Adoration	❑ Plenary ❑ Partial		❑ Chaplet ❑ Fm Tree
❑ Rosary ❑ Stations	❑ Scripture ❑ Adoration	❑ Plenary ❑ Partial		❑ Chaplet ❑ Fm Tree
❑ Rosary ❑ Stations	❑ Scripture ❑ Adoration	❑ Plenary ❑ Partial		❑ Chaplet ❑ Fm Tree
❑ Rosary ❑ Stations	❑ Scripture ❑ Adoration	❑ Plenary ❑ Partial		❑ Chaplet ❑ Fm Tree
❑ Rosary ❑ Stations	❑ Scripture ❑ Adoration	❑ Plenary ❑ Partial		❑ Chaplet ❑ Fm Tree
❑ Rosary ❑ Stations	❑ Scripture ❑ Adoration	❑ Plenary ❑ Partial		❑ Chaplet ❑ Fm Tree
❑ Rosary ❑ Stations	❑ Scripture ❑ Adoration	❑ Plenary ❑ Partial		❑ Chaplet ❑ Fm Tree
❑ Rosary ❑ Stations	❑ Scripture ❑ Adoration	❑ Plenary ❑ Partial		❑ Chaplet ❑ Fm Tree

SEARCH AND RESCUE

DATE	HOLY SOUL	SAINT

SEARCH AND RESCUE

OFFERING		PLENARY/ PARTIAL	COMRADE	DIVINE MERCY CHAPLET
❑ Rosary ❑ Stations	❑ Scripture ❑ Adoration	❑ Plenary ❑ Partial		❑ Chaplet ❑ Fm Tree
❑ Rosary ❑ Stations	❑ Scripture ❑ Adoration	❑ Plenary ❑ Partial		❑ Chaplet ❑ Fm Tree
❑ Rosary ❑ Stations	❑ Scripture ❑ Adoration	❑ Plenary ❑ Partial		❑ Chaplet ❑ Fm Tree
❑ Rosary ❑ Stations	❑ Scripture ❑ Adoration	❑ Plenary ❑ Partial		❑ Chaplet ❑ Fm Tree
❑ Rosary ❑ Stations	❑ Scripture ❑ Adoration	❑ Plenary ❑ Partial		❑ Chaplet ❑ Fm Tree
❑ Rosary ❑ Stations	❑ Scripture ❑ Adoration	❑ Plenary ❑ Partial		❑ Chaplet ❑ Fm Tree
❑ Rosary ❑ Stations	❑ Scripture ❑ Adoration	❑ Plenary ❑ Partial		❑ Chaplet ❑ Fm Tree
❑ Rosary ❑ Stations	❑ Scripture ❑ Adoration	❑ Plenary ❑ Partial		❑ Chaplet ❑ Fm Tree
❑ Rosary ❑ Stations	❑ Scripture ❑ Adoration	❑ Plenary ❑ Partial		❑ Chaplet ❑ Fm Tree
❑ Rosary ❑ Stations	❑ Scripture ❑ Adoration	❑ Plenary ❑ Partial		❑ Chaplet ❑ Fm Tree
❑ Rosary ❑ Stations	❑ Scripture ❑ Adoration	❑ Plenary ❑ Partial		❑ Chaplet ❑ Fm Tree
❑ Rosary ❑ Stations	❑ Scripture ❑ Adoration	❑ Plenary ❑ Partial		❑ Chaplet ❑ Fm Tree
❑ Rosary ❑ Stations	❑ Scripture ❑ Adoration	❑ Plenary ❑ Partial		❑ Chaplet ❑ Fm Tree
❑ Rosary ❑ Stations	❑ Scripture ❑ Adoration	❑ Plenary ❑ Partial		❑ Chaplet ❑ Fm Tree
❑ Rosary ❑ Stations	❑ Scripture ❑ Adoration	❑ Plenary ❑ Partial		❑ Chaplet ❑ Fm Tree
❑ Rosary ❑ Stations	❑ Scripture ❑ Adoration	❑ Plenary ❑ Partial		❑ Chaplet ❑ Fm Tree
❑ Rosary ❑ Stations	❑ Scripture ❑ Adoration	❑ Plenary ❑ Partial		❑ Chaplet ❑ Fm Tree
❑ Rosary ❑ Stations	❑ Scripture ❑ Adoration	❑ Plenary ❑ Partial		❑ Chaplet ❑ Fm Tree
❑ Rosary ❑ Stations	❑ Scripture ❑ Adoration	❑ Plenary ❑ Partial		❑ Chaplet ❑ Fm Tree
❑ Rosary ❑ Stations	❑ Scripture ❑ Adoration	❑ Plenary ❑ Partial		❑ Chaplet ❑ Fm Tree

SEARCH AND RESCUE

DATE	HOLY SOUL	SAINT

SEARCH AND RESCUE

OFFERING		PLENARY/ PARTIAL	COMRADE	DIVINE MERCY CHAPLET
❑ Rosary ❑ Stations	❑ Scripture ❑ Adoration	❑ Plenary ❑ Partial		❑ Chaplet ❑ Fm Tree
❑ Rosary ❑ Stations	❑ Scripture ❑ Adoration	❑ Plenary ❑ Partial		❑ Chaplet ❑ Fm Tree
❑ Rosary ❑ Stations	❑ Scripture ❑ Adoration	❑ Plenary ❑ Partial		❑ Chaplet ❑ Fm Tree
❑ Rosary ❑ Stations	❑ Scripture ❑ Adoration	❑ Plenary ❑ Partial		❑ Chaplet ❑ Fm Tree
❑ Rosary ❑ Stations	❑ Scripture ❑ Adoration	❑ Plenary ❑ Partial		❑ Chaplet ❑ Fm Tree
❑ Rosary ❑ Stations	❑ Scripture ❑ Adoration	❑ Plenary ❑ Partial		❑ Chaplet ❑ Fm Tree
❑ Rosary ❑ Stations	❑ Scripture ❑ Adoration	❑ Plenary ❑ Partial		❑ Chaplet ❑ Fm Tree
❑ Rosary ❑ Stations	❑ Scripture ❑ Adoration	❑ Plenary ❑ Partial		❑ Chaplet ❑ Fm Tree
❑ Rosary ❑ Stations	❑ Scripture ❑ Adoration	❑ Plenary ❑ Partial		❑ Chaplet ❑ Fm Tree
❑ Rosary ❑ Stations	❑ Scripture ❑ Adoration	❑ Plenary ❑ Partial		❑ Chaplet ❑ Fm Tree
❑ Rosary ❑ Stations	❑ Scripture ❑ Adoration	❑ Plenary ❑ Partial		❑ Chaplet ❑ Fm Tree
❑ Rosary ❑ Stations	❑ Scripture ❑ Adoration	❑ Plenary ❑ Partial		❑ Chaplet ❑ Fm Tree
❑ Rosary ❑ Stations	❑ Scripture ❑ Adoration	❑ Plenary ❑ Partial		❑ Chaplet ❑ Fm Tree
❑ Rosary ❑ Stations	❑ Scripture ❑ Adoration	❑ Plenary ❑ Partial		❑ Chaplet ❑ Fm Tree
❑ Rosary ❑ Stations	❑ Scripture ❑ Adoration	❑ Plenary ❑ Partial		❑ Chaplet ❑ Fm Tree
❑ Rosary ❑ Stations	❑ Scripture ❑ Adoration	❑ Plenary ❑ Partial		❑ Chaplet ❑ Fm Tree
❑ Rosary ❑ Stations	❑ Scripture ❑ Adoration	❑ Plenary ❑ Partial		❑ Chaplet ❑ Fm Tree
❑ Rosary ❑ Stations	❑ Scripture ❑ Adoration	❑ Plenary ❑ Partial		❑ Chaplet ❑ Fm Tree
❑ Rosary ❑ Stations	❑ Scripture ❑ Adoration	❑ Plenary ❑ Partial		❑ Chaplet ❑ Fm Tree
❑ Rosary ❑ Stations	❑ Scripture ❑ Adoration	❑ Plenary ❑ Partial		❑ Chaplet ❑ Fm Tree
❑ Rosary ❑ Stations	❑ Scripture ❑ Adoration	❑ Plenary ❑ Partial		❑ Chaplet ❑ Fm Tree
❑ Rosary ❑ Stations	❑ Scripture ❑ Adoration	❑ Plenary ❑ Partial		❑ Chaplet ❑ Fm Tree

SEARCH AND RESCUE

DATE	HOLY SOUL	SAINT

SEARCH AND RESCUE

OFFERING		PLENARY/ PARTIAL	COMRADE	DIVINE MERCY CHAPLET
❏ Rosary ❏ Stations	❏ Scripture ❏ Adoration	❏ Plenary ❏ Partial		❏ Chaplet ❏ Fm Tree
❏ Rosary ❏ Stations	❏ Scripture ❏ Adoration	❏ Plenary ❏ Partial		❏ Chaplet ❏ Fm Tree
❏ Rosary ❏ Stations	❏ Scripture ❏ Adoration	❏ Plenary ❏ Partial		❏ Chaplet ❏ Fm Tree
❏ Rosary ❏ Stations	❏ Scripture ❏ Adoration	❏ Plenary ❏ Partial		❏ Chaplet ❏ Fm Tree
❏ Rosary ❏ Stations	❏ Scripture ❏ Adoration	❏ Plenary ❏ Partial		❏ Chaplet ❏ Fm Tree
❏ Rosary ❏ Stations	❏ Scripture ❏ Adoration	❏ Plenary ❏ Partial		❏ Chaplet ❏ Fm Tree
❏ Rosary ❏ Stations	❏ Scripture ❏ Adoration	❏ Plenary ❏ Partial		❏ Chaplet ❏ Fm Tree
❏ Rosary ❏ Stations	❏ Scripture ❏ Adoration	❏ Plenary ❏ Partial		❏ Chaplet ❏ Fm Tree
❏ Rosary ❏ Stations	❏ Scripture ❏ Adoration	❏ Plenary ❏ Partial		❏ Chaplet ❏ Fm Tree
❏ Rosary ❏ Stations	❏ Scripture ❏ Adoration	❏ Plenary ❏ Partial		❏ Chaplet ❏ Fm Tree
❏ Rosary ❏ Stations	❏ Scripture ❏ Adoration	❏ Plenary ❏ Partial		❏ Chaplet ❏ Fm Tree
❏ Rosary ❏ Stations	❏ Scripture ❏ Adoration	❏ Plenary ❏ Partial		❏ Chaplet ❏ Fm Tree
❏ Rosary ❏ Stations	❏ Scripture ❏ Adoration	❏ Plenary ❏ Partial		❏ Chaplet ❏ Fm Tree
❏ Rosary ❏ Stations	❏ Scripture ❏ Adoration	❏ Plenary ❏ Partial		❏ Chaplet ❏ Fm Tree
❏ Rosary ❏ Stations	❏ Scripture ❏ Adoration	❏ Plenary ❏ Partial		❏ Chaplet ❏ Fm Tree
❏ Rosary ❏ Stations	❏ Scripture ❏ Adoration	❏ Plenary ❏ Partial		❏ Chaplet ❏ Fm Tree
❏ Rosary ❏ Stations	❏ Scripture ❏ Adoration	❏ Plenary ❏ Partial		❏ Chaplet ❏ Fm Tree
❏ Rosary ❏ Stations	❏ Scripture ❏ Adoration	❏ Plenary ❏ Partial		❏ Chaplet ❏ Fm Tree
❏ Rosary ❏ Stations	❏ Scripture ❏ Adoration	❏ Plenary ❏ Partial		❏ Chaplet ❏ Fm Tree
❏ Rosary ❏ Stations	❏ Scripture ❏ Adoration	❏ Plenary ❏ Partial		❏ Chaplet ❏ Fm Tree
❏ Rosary ❏ Stations	❏ Scripture ❏ Adoration	❏ Plenary ❏ Partial		❏ Chaplet ❏ Fm Tree

SEARCH AND RESCUE

DATE	HOLY SOUL	SAINT

SEARCH AND RESCUE

OFFERING		PLENARY/ PARTIAL	COMRADE	DIVINE MERCY CHAPLET
❏ Rosary ❏ Stations	❏ Scripture ❏ Adoration	❏ Plenary ❏ Partial		❏ Chaplet ❏ Fm Tree
❏ Rosary ❏ Stations	❏ Scripture ❏ Adoration	❏ Plenary ❏ Partial		❏ Chaplet ❏ Fm Tree
❏ Rosary ❏ Stations	❏ Scripture ❏ Adoration	❏ Plenary ❏ Partial		❏ Chaplet ❏ Fm Tree
❏ Rosary ❏ Stations	❏ Scripture ❏ Adoration	❏ Plenary ❏ Partial		❏ Chaplet ❏ Fm Tree
❏ Rosary ❏ Stations	❏ Scripture ❏ Adoration	❏ Plenary ❏ Partial		❏ Chaplet ❏ Fm Tree
❏ Rosary ❏ Stations	❏ Scripture ❏ Adoration	❏ Plenary ❏ Partial		❏ Chaplet ❏ Fm Tree
❏ Rosary ❏ Stations	❏ Scripture ❏ Adoration	❏ Plenary ❏ Partial		❏ Chaplet ❏ Fm Tree
❏ Rosary ❏ Stations	❏ Scripture ❏ Adoration	❏ Plenary ❏ Partial		❏ Chaplet ❏ Fm Tree
❏ Rosary ❏ Stations	❏ Scripture ❏ Adoration	❏ Plenary ❏ Partial		❏ Chaplet ❏ Fm Tree
❏ Rosary ❏ Stations	❏ Scripture ❏ Adoration	❏ Plenary ❏ Partial		❏ Chaplet ❏ Fm Tree
❏ Rosary ❏ Stations	❏ Scripture ❏ Adoration	❏ Plenary ❏ Partial		❏ Chaplet ❏ Fm Tree
❏ Rosary ❏ Stations	❏ Scripture ❏ Adoration	❏ Plenary ❏ Partial		❏ Chaplet ❏ Fm Tree
❏ Rosary ❏ Stations	❏ Scripture ❏ Adoration	❏ Plenary ❏ Partial		❏ Chaplet ❏ Fm Tree
❏ Rosary ❏ Stations	❏ Scripture ❏ Adoration	❏ Plenary ❏ Partial		❏ Chaplet ❏ Fm Tree
❏ Rosary ❏ Stations	❏ Scripture ❏ Adoration	❏ Plenary ❏ Partial		❏ Chaplet ❏ Fm Tree
❏ Rosary ❏ Stations	❏ Scripture ❏ Adoration	❏ Plenary ❏ Partial		❏ Chaplet ❏ Fm Tree
❏ Rosary ❏ Stations	❏ Scripture ❏ Adoration	❏ Plenary ❏ Partial		❏ Chaplet ❏ Fm Tree
❏ Rosary ❏ Stations	❏ Scripture ❏ Adoration	❏ Plenary ❏ Partial		❏ Chaplet ❏ Fm Tree
❏ Rosary ❏ Stations	❏ Scripture ❏ Adoration	❏ Plenary ❏ Partial		❏ Chaplet ❏ Fm Tree
❏ Rosary ❏ Stations	❏ Scripture ❏ Adoration	❏ Plenary ❏ Partial		❏ Chaplet ❏ Fm Tree
❏ Rosary ❏ Stations	❏ Scripture ❏ Adoration	❏ Plenary ❏ Partial		❏ Chaplet ❏ Fm Tree

SEARCH AND RESCUE

DATE	HOLY SOUL	SAINT

SEARCH AND RESCUE

OFFERING		PLENARY/ PARTIAL	COMRADE	DIVINE MERCY CHAPLET
❏ Rosary ❏ Stations	❏ Scripture ❏ Adoration	❏ Plenary ❏ Partial		❏ Chaplet ❏ Fm Tree
❏ Rosary ❏ Stations	❏ Scripture ❏ Adoration	❏ Plenary ❏ Partial		❏ Chaplet ❏ Fm Tree
❏ Rosary ❏ Stations	❏ Scripture ❏ Adoration	❏ Plenary ❏ Partial		❏ Chaplet ❏ Fm Tree
❏ Rosary ❏ Stations	❏ Scripture ❏ Adoration	❏ Plenary ❏ Partial		❏ Chaplet ❏ Fm Tree
❏ Rosary ❏ Stations	❏ Scripture ❏ Adoration	❏ Plenary ❏ Partial		❏ Chaplet ❏ Fm Tree
❏ Rosary ❏ Stations	❏ Scripture ❏ Adoration	❏ Plenary ❏ Partial		❏ Chaplet ❏ Fm Tree
❏ Rosary ❏ Stations	❏ Scripture ❏ Adoration	❏ Plenary ❏ Partial		❏ Chaplet ❏ Fm Tree
❏ Rosary ❏ Stations	❏ Scripture ❏ Adoration	❏ Plenary ❏ Partial		❏ Chaplet ❏ Fm Tree
❏ Rosary ❏ Stations	❏ Scripture ❏ Adoration	❏ Plenary ❏ Partial		❏ Chaplet ❏ Fm Tree
❏ Rosary ❏ Stations	❏ Scripture ❏ Adoration	❏ Plenary ❏ Partial		❏ Chaplet ❏ Fm Tree
❏ Rosary ❏ Stations	❏ Scripture ❏ Adoration	❏ Plenary ❏ Partial		❏ Chaplet ❏ Fm Tree
❏ Rosary ❏ Stations	❏ Scripture ❏ Adoration	❏ Plenary ❏ Partial		❏ Chaplet ❏ Fm Tree
❏ Rosary ❏ Stations	❏ Scripture ❏ Adoration	❏ Plenary ❏ Partial		❏ Chaplet ❏ Fm Tree
❏ Rosary ❏ Stations	❏ Scripture ❏ Adoration	❏ Plenary ❏ Partial		❏ Chaplet ❏ Fm Tree
❏ Rosary ❏ Stations	❏ Scripture ❏ Adoration	❏ Plenary ❏ Partial		❏ Chaplet ❏ Fm Tree
❏ Rosary ❏ Stations	❏ Scripture ❏ Adoration	❏ Plenary ❏ Partial		❏ Chaplet ❏ Fm Tree
❏ Rosary ❏ Stations	❏ Scripture ❏ Adoration	❏ Plenary ❏ Partial		❏ Chaplet ❏ Fm Tree
❏ Rosary ❏ Stations	❏ Scripture ❏ Adoration	❏ Plenary ❏ Partial		❏ Chaplet ❏ Fm Tree
❏ Rosary ❏ Stations	❏ Scripture ❏ Adoration	❏ Plenary ❏ Partial		❏ Chaplet ❏ Fm Tree
❏ Rosary ❏ Stations	❏ Scripture ❏ Adoration	❏ Plenary ❏ Partial		❏ Chaplet ❏ Fm Tree
❏ Rosary ❏ Stations	❏ Scripture ❏ Adoration	❏ Plenary ❏ Partial		❏ Chaplet ❏ Fm Tree

SEARCH AND RESCUE

DATE	HOLY SOUL	SAINT

SEARCH AND RESCUE

OFFERING		PLENARY/ PARTIAL	COMRADE	DIVINE MERCY CHAPLET
❑ Rosary ❑ Stations	❑ Scripture ❑ Adoration	❑ Plenary ❑ Partial		❑ Chaplet ❑ Fm Tree
❑ Rosary ❑ Stations	❑ Scripture ❑ Adoration	❑ Plenary ❑ Partial		❑ Chaplet ❑ Fm Tree
❑ Rosary ❑ Stations	❑ Scripture ❑ Adoration	❑ Plenary ❑ Partial		❑ Chaplet ❑ Fm Tree
❑ Rosary ❑ Stations	❑ Scripture ❑ Adoration	❑ Plenary ❑ Partial		❑ Chaplet ❑ Fm Tree
❑ Rosary ❑ Stations	❑ Scripture ❑ Adoration	❑ Plenary ❑ Partial		❑ Chaplet ❑ Fm Tree
❑ Rosary ❑ Stations	❑ Scripture ❑ Adoration	❑ Plenary ❑ Partial		❑ Chaplet ❑ Fm Tree
❑ Rosary ❑ Stations	❑ Scripture ❑ Adoration	❑ Plenary ❑ Partial		❑ Chaplet ❑ Fm Tree
❑ Rosary ❑ Stations	❑ Scripture ❑ Adoration	❑ Plenary ❑ Partial		❑ Chaplet ❑ Fm Tree
❑ Rosary ❑ Stations	❑ Scripture ❑ Adoration	❑ Plenary ❑ Partial		❑ Chaplet ❑ Fm Tree
❑ Rosary ❑ Stations	❑ Scripture ❑ Adoration	❑ Plenary ❑ Partial		❑ Chaplet ❑ Fm Tree
❑ Rosary ❑ Stations	❑ Scripture ❑ Adoration	❑ Plenary ❑ Partial		❑ Chaplet ❑ Fm Tree
❑ Rosary ❑ Stations	❑ Scripture ❑ Adoration	❑ Plenary ❑ Partial		❑ Chaplet ❑ Fm Tree
❑ Rosary ❑ Stations	❑ Scripture ❑ Adoration	❑ Plenary ❑ Partial		❑ Chaplet ❑ Fm Tree
❑ Rosary ❑ Stations	❑ Scripture ❑ Adoration	❑ Plenary ❑ Partial		❑ Chaplet ❑ Fm Tree
❑ Rosary ❑ Stations	❑ Scripture ❑ Adoration	❑ Plenary ❑ Partial		❑ Chaplet ❑ Fm Tree
❑ Rosary ❑ Stations	❑ Scripture ❑ Adoration	❑ Plenary ❑ Partial		❑ Chaplet ❑ Fm Tree
❑ Rosary ❑ Stations	❑ Scripture ❑ Adoration	❑ Plenary ❑ Partial		❑ Chaplet ❑ Fm Tree
❑ Rosary ❑ Stations	❑ Scripture ❑ Adoration	❑ Plenary ❑ Partial		❑ Chaplet ❑ Fm Tree
❑ Rosary ❑ Stations	❑ Scripture ❑ Adoration	❑ Plenary ❑ Partial		❑ Chaplet ❑ Fm Tree
❑ Rosary ❑ Stations	❑ Scripture ❑ Adoration	❑ Plenary ❑ Partial		❑ Chaplet ❑ Fm Tree
❑ Rosary ❑ Stations	❑ Scripture ❑ Adoration	❑ Plenary ❑ Partial		❑ Chaplet ❑ Fm Tree

JOURNAL TWO: PRAYER REQUESTS

Pray for Others with Padre Pio Power!

"Prayer is the most potent force known to humanity. Because we have been made partakers in Jesus' victory over sin and death (1 Jn 4:4), we have the authority as sons and daughters of God to pray for others, pushing back the darkness of sin and oppression. In prayer, we have a weapon that has "divine power to destroy strongholds" (2 Cor 10:4). That kind of weaponry — the power of prayer — is something God invites us to use as we seek not only personal transformation but the transformation of the world as well. An intercessor is one who takes up a "burden" that goes far beyond his or her own needs and intentions."[13] — That is how *Partners in Evangelism* describes the immense power of prayer.

When someone asks you to pray for them, why not pray with "Padre Pio Power"? When I heard that the prayer below (written by St. Margaret Mary Alacoque) was the one Padre Pio would use when people asked him to pray for them, I needed no further encouragement for choosing this prayer in the same way. Padre Pio has tens of thousands of miracles associated with him, including the healing of a very good friend of Pope John Paul II.

A convenient journal section has been created to record these special intentions. Keep in mind this type of petition is for specific needs such as gainful employment or healing from an illness. After some time has passed, refer back to this journal to record the amazing way God answers these prayers. Due to our limited view and God's eternal view, it is important to always trust that He knows far better what is really needed in these situations. Be open to seeing how sometimes He answers our specific prayers in a way that does not always match exactly with what we asked. When looking back on these petitions, see how His way is better.

Padre Pio's Sacred Heart Novena Prayer

O my Jesus, You have said: "Truly I say to you, ask and you will receive, seek and you will find, knock and it will be opened to you." Behold I knock, I seek and ask for the grace of *(here name your request)*. Our Father ... Hail Mary ... Glory Be ... Sacred Heart of Jesus, I place all my trust in You.

O my Jesus, You have said: "Truly I say to you, if you ask anything of the Father in My name, He will give it to you." Behold, in Your name, I ask the Father for the grace of *(here name your request)*. Our Father ... Hail Mary ... Glory Be ... Sacred Heart of Jesus, I place all my trust in You.

O my Jesus, You have said: "Truly I say to you, heaven and earth will pass away but My words will not pass away." Encouraged by Your infallible words I now ask for the grace of *(here name your request)*. Our Father ... Hail Mary ... Glory Be ... Sacred Heart of Jesus, I place all my trust in You.

O Sacred Heart of Jesus, for whom it is impossible not to have compassion on the afflicted, have pity on us miserable sinners and grant us the grace which we ask of You, through the Sorrowful and Immaculate Heart of Mary, Your tender Mother and ours.

Say the Hail, Holy Queen and add: "St. Joseph, foster father of Jesus, pray for us."

How to use the Prayer Requests Journal

1. Write the name of the person who is in need of a special prayer in the COMRADE IN NEED column.

2. Write your specific prayer request for them in the PRAYER REQUEST column. Keep in mind these intentions are generally more specific than a person's spiritual conversion. Pray the Sacred Heart Novena Prayer and place a checkmark next to PIO PRAYER.

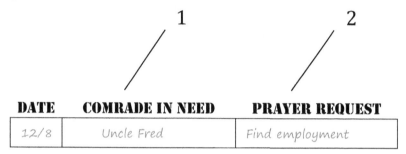

DATE	COMRADE IN NEED	PRAYER REQUEST
12/8	Uncle Fred	Find employment

3. After some time has passed, write how God answered these prayers in the GLORY REPORT column. Always keep in mind that God knows best what is needed in a given situation to fulfill our ultimate goal of being with Him in heaven.

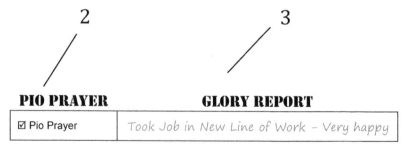

PIO PRAYER	GLORY REPORT
☑ Pio Prayer	Took Job in New Line of Work – Very happy

PRAYER REQUESTS JOURNAL

PRAYER REQUESTS

DATE	COMRADE IN NEED	PRAYER REQUEST

PRAYER REQUESTS

PIO PRAYER	GLORY REPORT
❏ Pio Prayer	
❏ Pio Prayer	
❏ Pio Prayer	
❏ Pio Prayer	
❏ Pio Prayer	
❏ Pio Prayer	
❏ Pio Prayer	
❏ Pio Prayer	
❏ Pio Prayer	
❏ Pio Prayer	
❏ Pio Prayer	
❏ Pio Prayer	
❏ Pio Prayer	
❏ Pio Prayer	
❏ Pio Prayer	
❏ Pio Prayer	
❏ Pio Prayer	
❏ Pio Prayer	
❏ Pio Prayer	
❏ Pio Prayer	
❏ Pio Prayer	

PRAYER REQUESTS

DATE	COMRADE IN NEED	PRAYER REQUEST

PRAYER REQUESTS

PIO PRAYER   GLORY REPORT

PIO PRAYER	GLORY REPORT
❏ Pio Prayer	
❏ Pio Prayer	
❏ Pio Prayer	
❏ Pio Prayer	
❏ Pio Prayer	
❏ Pio Prayer	
❏ Pio Prayer	
❏ Pio Prayer	
❏ Pio Prayer	
❏ Pio Prayer	
❏ Pio Prayer	
❏ Pio Prayer	
❏ Pio Prayer	
❏ Pio Prayer	
❏ Pio Prayer	
❏ Pio Prayer	
❏ Pio Prayer	
❏ Pio Prayer	
❏ Pio Prayer	
❏ Pio Prayer	
❏ Pio Prayer	

PRAYER REQUESTS

DATE	COMRADE IN NEED	PRAYER REQUEST

PRAYER REQUESTS

PIO PRAYER	GLORY REPORT
❑ Pio Prayer	
❑ Pio Prayer	
❑ Pio Prayer	
❑ Pio Prayer	
❑ Pio Prayer	
❑ Pio Prayer	
❑ Pio Prayer	
❑ Pio Prayer	
❑ Pio Prayer	
❑ Pio Prayer	
❑ Pio Prayer	
❑ Pio Prayer	
❑ Pio Prayer	
❑ Pio Prayer	
❑ Pio Prayer	
❑ Pio Prayer	
❑ Pio Prayer	
❑ Pio Prayer	
❑ Pio Prayer	
❑ Pio Prayer	
❑ Pio Prayer	

PRAYER REQUESTS

DATE	COMRADE IN NEED	PRAYER REQUEST

PRAYER REQUESTS

PIO PRAYER	GLORY REPORT
❑ Pio Prayer	
❑ Pio Prayer	
❑ Pio Prayer	
❑ Pio Prayer	
❑ Pio Prayer	
❑ Pio Prayer	
❑ Pio Prayer	
❑ Pio Prayer	
❑ Pio Prayer	
❑ Pio Prayer	
❑ Pio Prayer	
❑ Pio Prayer	
❑ Pio Prayer	
❑ Pio Prayer	
❑ Pio Prayer	
❑ Pio Prayer	
❑ Pio Prayer	
❑ Pio Prayer	
❑ Pio Prayer	
❑ Pio Prayer	
❑ Pio Prayer	

PRAYER REQUESTS

DATE	COMRADE IN NEED	PRAYER REQUEST

PRAYER REQUESTS

PIO PRAYER	GLORY REPORT
❑ Pio Prayer	
❑ Pio Prayer	
❑ Pio Prayer	
❑ Pio Prayer	
❑ Pio Prayer	
❑ Pio Prayer	
❑ Pio Prayer	
❑ Pio Prayer	
❑ Pio Prayer	
❑ Pio Prayer	
❑ Pio Prayer	
❑ Pio Prayer	
❑ Pio Prayer	
❑ Pio Prayer	
❑ Pio Prayer	
❑ Pio Prayer	
❑ Pio Prayer	
❑ Pio Prayer	
❑ Pio Prayer	
❑ Pio Prayer	
❑ Pio Prayer	

PRAYER REQUESTS

DATE	COMRADE IN NEED	PRAYER REQUEST

PRAYER REQUESTS

PIO PRAYER	GLORY REPORT
❑ Pio Prayer	
❑ Pio Prayer	
❑ Pio Prayer	
❑ Pio Prayer	
❑ Pio Prayer	
❑ Pio Prayer	
❑ Pio Prayer	
❑ Pio Prayer	
❑ Pio Prayer	
❑ Pio Prayer	
❑ Pio Prayer	
❑ Pio Prayer	
❑ Pio Prayer	
❑ Pio Prayer	
❑ Pio Prayer	
❑ Pio Prayer	
❑ Pio Prayer	
❑ Pio Prayer	
❑ Pio Prayer	
❑ Pio Prayer	
❑ Pio Prayer	

PRAYER REQUESTS

DATE	COMRADE IN NEED	PRAYER REQUEST

PRAYER REQUESTS

PIO PRAYER	GLORY REPORT
❑ Pio Prayer	
❑ Pio Prayer	
❑ Pio Prayer	
❑ Pio Prayer	
❑ Pio Prayer	
❑ Pio Prayer	
❑ Pio Prayer	
❑ Pio Prayer	
❑ Pio Prayer	
❑ Pio Prayer	
❑ Pio Prayer	
❑ Pio Prayer	
❑ Pio Prayer	
❑ Pio Prayer	
❑ Pio Prayer	
❑ Pio Prayer	
❑ Pio Prayer	
❑ Pio Prayer	
❑ Pio Prayer	
❑ Pio Prayer	
❑ Pio Prayer	

PRAYER REQUESTS

DATE	COMRADE IN NEED	PRAYER REQUEST

PRAYER REQUESTS

PIO PRAYER	GLORY REPORT
❑ Pio Prayer	
❑ Pio Prayer	
❑ Pio Prayer	
❑ Pio Prayer	
❑ Pio Prayer	
❑ Pio Prayer	
❑ Pio Prayer	
❑ Pio Prayer	
❑ Pio Prayer	
❑ Pio Prayer	
❑ Pio Prayer	
❑ Pio Prayer	
❑ Pio Prayer	
❑ Pio Prayer	
❑ Pio Prayer	
❑ Pio Prayer	
❑ Pio Prayer	
❑ Pio Prayer	
❑ Pio Prayer	
❑ Pio Prayer	
❑ Pio Prayer	
❑ Pio Prayer	

PRAYER REQUESTS

DATE	COMRADE IN NEED	PRAYER REQUEST

PRAYER REQUESTS

PIO PRAYER	GLORY REPORT
❑ Pio Prayer	
❑ Pio Prayer	
❑ Pio Prayer	
❑ Pio Prayer	
❑ Pio Prayer	
❑ Pio Prayer	
❑ Pio Prayer	
❑ Pio Prayer	
❑ Pio Prayer	
❑ Pio Prayer	
❑ Pio Prayer	
❑ Pio Prayer	
❑ Pio Prayer	
❑ Pio Prayer	
❑ Pio Prayer	
❑ Pio Prayer	
❑ Pio Prayer	
❑ Pio Prayer	
❑ Pio Prayer	
❑ Pio Prayer	
❑ Pio Prayer	
❑ Pio Prayer	

PRAYER REQUESTS

DATE	COMRADE IN NEED	PRAYER REQUEST

PRAYER REQUESTS

PIO PRAYER	GLORY REPORT
❏ Pio Prayer	
❏ Pio Prayer	
❏ Pio Prayer	
❏ Pio Prayer	
❏ Pio Prayer	
❏ Pio Prayer	
❏ Pio Prayer	
❏ Pio Prayer	
❏ Pio Prayer	
❏ Pio Prayer	
❏ Pio Prayer	
❏ Pio Prayer	
❏ Pio Prayer	
❏ Pio Prayer	
❏ Pio Prayer	
❏ Pio Prayer	
❏ Pio Prayer	
❏ Pio Prayer	
❏ Pio Prayer	
❏ Pio Prayer	
❏ Pio Prayer	

PRAYER REQUESTS

DATE	COMRADE IN NEED	PRAYER REQUEST

PRAYER REQUESTS

PIO PRAYER	GLORY REPORT
❑ Pio Prayer	
❑ Pio Prayer	
❑ Pio Prayer	
❑ Pio Prayer	
❑ Pio Prayer	
❑ Pio Prayer	
❑ Pio Prayer	
❑ Pio Prayer	
❑ Pio Prayer	
❑ Pio Prayer	
❑ Pio Prayer	
❑ Pio Prayer	
❑ Pio Prayer	
❑ Pio Prayer	
❑ Pio Prayer	
❑ Pio Prayer	
❑ Pio Prayer	
❑ Pio Prayer	
❑ Pio Prayer	
❑ Pio Prayer	
❑ Pio Prayer	

PRAYER REQUESTS

DATE	COMRADE IN NEED	PRAYER REQUEST

PRAYER REQUESTS

PIO PRAYER	GLORY REPORT
❏ Pio Prayer	
❏ Pio Prayer	
❏ Pio Prayer	
❏ Pio Prayer	
❏ Pio Prayer	
❏ Pio Prayer	
❏ Pio Prayer	
❏ Pio Prayer	
❏ Pio Prayer	
❏ Pio Prayer	
❏ Pio Prayer	
❏ Pio Prayer	
❏ Pio Prayer	
❏ Pio Prayer	
❏ Pio Prayer	
❏ Pio Prayer	
❏ Pio Prayer	
❏ Pio Prayer	
❏ Pio Prayer	
❏ Pio Prayer	
❏ Pio Prayer	

PRAYER REQUESTS

DATE	COMRADE IN NEED	PRAYER REQUEST

PRAYER REQUESTS

PIO PRAYER	GLORY REPORT
❑ Pio Prayer	
❑ Pio Prayer	
❑ Pio Prayer	
❑ Pio Prayer	
❑ Pio Prayer	
❑ Pio Prayer	
❑ Pio Prayer	
❑ Pio Prayer	
❑ Pio Prayer	
❑ Pio Prayer	
❑ Pio Prayer	
❑ Pio Prayer	
❑ Pio Prayer	
❑ Pio Prayer	
❑ Pio Prayer	
❑ Pio Prayer	
❑ Pio Prayer	
❑ Pio Prayer	
❑ Pio Prayer	
❑ Pio Prayer	
❑ Pio Prayer	

PRAYER REQUESTS

DATE	COMRADE IN NEED	PRAYER REQUEST

PRAYER REQUESTS

PIO PRAYER
GLORY REPORT

PIO PRAYER	GLORY REPORT
❑ Pio Prayer	
❑ Pio Prayer	
❑ Pio Prayer	
❑ Pio Prayer	
❑ Pio Prayer	
❑ Pio Prayer	
❑ Pio Prayer	
❑ Pio Prayer	
❑ Pio Prayer	
❑ Pio Prayer	
❑ Pio Prayer	
❑ Pio Prayer	
❑ Pio Prayer	
❑ Pio Prayer	
❑ Pio Prayer	
❑ Pio Prayer	
❑ Pio Prayer	
❑ Pio Prayer	
❑ Pio Prayer	
❑ Pio Prayer	
❑ Pio Prayer	

PRAYER REQUESTS

DATE	COMRADE IN NEED	PRAYER REQUEST

PRAYER REQUESTS

PIO PRAYER	GLORY REPORT
❑ Pio Prayer	
❑ Pio Prayer	
❑ Pio Prayer	
❑ Pio Prayer	
❑ Pio Prayer	
❑ Pio Prayer	
❑ Pio Prayer	
❑ Pio Prayer	
❑ Pio Prayer	
❑ Pio Prayer	
❑ Pio Prayer	
❑ Pio Prayer	
❑ Pio Prayer	
❑ Pio Prayer	
❑ Pio Prayer	
❑ Pio Prayer	
❑ Pio Prayer	
❑ Pio Prayer	
❑ Pio Prayer	
❑ Pio Prayer	
❑ Pio Prayer	

PRAYER REQUESTS

DATE	COMRADE IN NEED	PRAYER REQUEST

PRAYER REQUESTS

PIO PRAYER	GLORY REPORT
❏ Pio Prayer	
❏ Pio Prayer	
❏ Pio Prayer	
❏ Pio Prayer	
❏ Pio Prayer	
❏ Pio Prayer	
❏ Pio Prayer	
❏ Pio Prayer	
❏ Pio Prayer	
❏ Pio Prayer	
❏ Pio Prayer	
❏ Pio Prayer	
❏ Pio Prayer	
❏ Pio Prayer	
❏ Pio Prayer	
❏ Pio Prayer	
❏ Pio Prayer	
❏ Pio Prayer	
❏ Pio Prayer	
❏ Pio Prayer	
❏ Pio Prayer	

PRAYER REQUESTS

DATE	COMRADE IN NEED	PRAYER REQUEST

106

PRAYER REQUESTS

PIO PRAYER	GLORY REPORT
❏ Pio Prayer	
❏ Pio Prayer	
❏ Pio Prayer	
❏ Pio Prayer	
❏ Pio Prayer	
❏ Pio Prayer	
❏ Pio Prayer	
❏ Pio Prayer	
❏ Pio Prayer	
❏ Pio Prayer	
❏ Pio Prayer	
❏ Pio Prayer	
❏ Pio Prayer	
❏ Pio Prayer	
❏ Pio Prayer	
❏ Pio Prayer	
❏ Pio Prayer	
❏ Pio Prayer	
❏ Pio Prayer	
❏ Pio Prayer	
❏ Pio Prayer	

PRAYER REQUESTS

DATE	COMRADE IN NEED	PRAYER REQUEST

PRAYER REQUESTS

PIO PRAYER	GLORY REPORT
❏ Pio Prayer	
❏ Pio Prayer	
❏ Pio Prayer	
❏ Pio Prayer	
❏ Pio Prayer	
❏ Pio Prayer	
❏ Pio Prayer	
❏ Pio Prayer	
❏ Pio Prayer	
❏ Pio Prayer	
❏ Pio Prayer	
❏ Pio Prayer	
❏ Pio Prayer	
❏ Pio Prayer	
❏ Pio Prayer	
❏ Pio Prayer	
❏ Pio Prayer	
❏ Pio Prayer	
❏ Pio Prayer	
❏ Pio Prayer	
❏ Pio Prayer	

PRAYER REQUESTS

DATE	COMRADE IN NEED	PRAYER REQUEST

PRAYER REQUESTS

PIO PRAYER	GLORY REPORT
❏ Pio Prayer	
❏ Pio Prayer	
❏ Pio Prayer	
❏ Pio Prayer	
❏ Pio Prayer	
❏ Pio Prayer	
❏ Pio Prayer	
❏ Pio Prayer	
❏ Pio Prayer	
❏ Pio Prayer	
❏ Pio Prayer	
❏ Pio Prayer	
❏ Pio Prayer	
❏ Pio Prayer	
❏ Pio Prayer	
❏ Pio Prayer	
❏ Pio Prayer	
❏ Pio Prayer	
❏ Pio Prayer	
❏ Pio Prayer	
❏ Pio Prayer	

PRAYER REQUESTS

DATE	COMRADE IN NEED	PRAYER REQUEST

PRAYER REQUESTS

PIO PRAYER   GLORY REPORT

❏ Pio Prayer	
❏ Pio Prayer	
❏ Pio Prayer	
❏ Pio Prayer	
❏ Pio Prayer	
❏ Pio Prayer	
❏ Pio Prayer	
❏ Pio Prayer	
❏ Pio Prayer	
❏ Pio Prayer	
❏ Pio Prayer	
❏ Pio Prayer	
❏ Pio Prayer	
❏ Pio Prayer	
❏ Pio Prayer	
❏ Pio Prayer	
❏ Pio Prayer	
❏ Pio Prayer	
❏ Pio Prayer	
❏ Pio Prayer	
❏ Pio Prayer	

JOURNAL THREE: CHURCH MILITANT BOOT CAMP

"You shall love the Lord your God with all your heart, and with all your soul, and with all your mind, and with all your strength." — Mark 12:30

"He must increase, but I must decrease" (Jn 3:30). St. John the Baptist knew his mission was not about himself but to prepare the way of the Lord. In the same way, we who are called to be warrior saints need to grow in our understanding that it is not about "me," it is about God and His mission of saving souls.

In the U.S. Army's Basic Combat Training, the first goal of the drill sergeants is to get everyone working and functioning as a team so they can accomplish the goals set before them. This is why one of the first phases of the training includes shaving all heads, as all recruits wear the same uniform. Why? Because there can be no elitism and no stereotypes if they are to work together as a team, a unified fighting force.

Real love — heroic love — is selfless; it is not egocentric, but absolutely self-emptying, as we identify in the supreme sacrifice of love in our crucified Lord and Savior, Jesus Christ. Similarly, the accounts of military bravery usually include a soldier's willingness to put himself in harm's way while he places the welfare of his comrades ahead of his own safety and security.

This is what St. Paul was getting at when he wrote: "I have been crucified with Christ; it is no longer I who live, but Christ who lives in me; and the life I now live in the flesh I live in the Son of God, Who loved me and gave Himself for me" (Gal 2:20). We Christians-in-training are forever looking for opportunities to empty ourselves in order to allow Christ to fill us.

This is why the Church Militant Boot Camp looks no further than the four facets of love Christ identified as the summation of the entire law and the prophets: "You shall love the Lord your God with all your heart, and with all your soul, and with all your mind, and with all your strength" (Mk 12:30). And then to understand that the second great commandment — "You shall love your neighbor as yourself" — is the natural consequence and result of the first, because a person who genuinely loves God also loves others because he knows we are all brothers and sisters, children of the same Father.

Heart

Love the Lord your God with all your heart: What is our first priority? Where does our heart lie? If we are consumed by thoughts of the next meeting or problem or bill, then our heart is in the wrong place. It takes great faith to trust Jesus who said, "Seek first the kingdom of God and His righteousness, and all these things will be given you besides" (Mt 6:33), yet He has remained faithful to those words time and time again.

To seek first the kingdom of God is to seek what matters most to God, and that is souls. To love God with all your heart means to strive to have the heart of God. It is a heart that burns for souls. From the Diary of St.

Faustina, our Lord tells us, "Zeal for the salvation of souls should burn in our hearts" (Diary 350).

Recall that you have been commissioned an officer in the Church Militant. This means that your love and concern is initiated through the powers of the offices we receive in Baptism: priest, prophet, and king. As we said, you will want to hone your skills for sharing with loved ones the hope that is within you (prophet), and you will want to cheerfully accept every opportunity and challenge to bravely demonstrate your resolve to place the kingdom of God first in your life (king). You'll want to be strong in God's grace and well prepared when situations such as these arise for you to deploy these actions.

But, intercessory prayer and sacrifice (priest) is something we can actually schedule into our daily lives, especially as we have learned that every day we are gifted with a chance to offer one plenary indulgence (and only one) for a deceased loved one. We also learned that we could then ask our amassing Holy Alliance to join us in prayer for a living soul to receive the supernatural grace of faith, hope, and love. Finally, every day can be a day to offer our prayers for those with other needs (health, work, etc.).

Recommendations: Follow the directions on page 23 for your daily mission of search and rescue for a holy soul in purgatory and a fellow comrade in the Church Militant you feel could use God's amazing breakthrough of grace. In the Prayers of Petition section starting on page 69, keep track of those you pray for who have other kinds of needs.

Soul

Love the Lord your God with all your soul: The Catechism of the Catholic Church teaches that while the human person, created in the image of God, is a being at once corporeal and spiritual, the "soul also refers to the innermost aspect of man, that which is of greatest value in him, that by which he is most especially in God's image: 'soul' signifies the *spiritual principle* in man" (CCC 363).

Pope John Paul II extended an invitation to all of us during the canonization of St. Josemaria Escriva: "'Put out into the deep,' the divine Teacher says to us, 'and let down your nets for a catch' (Lk 5:4). To fulfill such a rigorous mission, one needs constant interior growth nourished by prayer. St. Josemaria was a master in the practice of prayer, which he considered to be an extraordinary 'weapon' to redeem the world. He always recommended: 'In the first place prayer; then expiation; in the third place, but very much in third place, action' (*The Way*, n. 82). It is not a paradox but a perennial truth: the fruitfulness of the apostolate lies above all in prayer and in intense and constant sacramental life. This, in essence, is the secret of the holiness and the true success of the saints."[14]

Recommendations: Over the course of the boot camp, slowly incorporate the Seven Daily Habits for Holy Apostolic People as outlined on page 18. In two-week increments, add one or two of these habits.

Mind

Love the Lord your God with all your mind: All of us are in spiritual darkness, to some degree. Jesus comes as light and truth. When there is a breakthrough of grace, we see everything differently and we have different aspirations. The Divine Life transforms our natural propensity for wealth, pleasure, power, and honor. There is a breakthrough of a new world, God's life, and a new perspective breaks in. It is amazing to witness a soul who has received this incredible gift. At once, there is an unquenchable thirst to know God more.

We must pray for this amazing breakthrough of grace, but we must also position ourselves in the best place for receiving this gift. That is why this Church Militant Boot Camp has recruits begin by turning to some very powerful devotional books that ask us to reflect upon only a few sentences each day. By beginning with these bite-sized portions of spiritual reading, recruits will begin to notice their hearts being prepared for this breakthrough of grace.

Recommendations: I highly recommend starting your boot camp with the *Preparation for Total Consecration* by St. Louis de Montfort. This consecration to Jesus through Mary is a great way to call out to God for that breakthrough of grace. It has very short daily reflections over a 33-day period. Other powerful daily devotionals are *My Daily Bread* by Fr. Anthony Paone, the *Diary of St. Faustina,* and *The Imitation of Christ* by Thomas à Kempis. Visit *http://churchmilitant.com/reading-plan/* for a list of 100 books considered by Fr. John McCloskey to constitute a Catholic Lifetime Reading Plan.

Strength

Love the Lord your God with all your strength: In *Gaudium et Spes* of the Council of Vatican II we read, "Man, though made of body and soul, is a unity. Through his very bodily condition he sums up in himself the elements of the material world. Through him they are thus brought to their highest perfection and can raise their voice in praise freely given to the Creator. For this reason man may not despise his bodily life. Rather he is obliged to regard his body as good and to hold it in honor since God has created it and will raise it up on the last day."[15]

We have a tendency to disconnect the pieces of our life — work, exercise, prayer — but it is usually true that if we are flabby, our faith tends to be flabby. God has a real purpose for our lives, and it certainly is not true that God wills that it be hindered by frequent illnesses and fatigue.

Our "will" is that spiritual power of the soul by which we choose to do something. While fasting and abstinence are traditional forms of mortification of the flesh, why not add the challenge of a fitness regimen as an excellent way to, as we say in the Catholic world, "offer it up"? Certainly the discipline of diet and exercise will accomplish the goals of mortification, which is to die to the control worldly desires have over our lives. This is the true goal when we talk about "loving the Lord your God with all your strength."

Recommendation: *Body for Life* is outstanding for beginners or veterans. You can order the book and journal online and/or use their website. Tony Horton's *Power 90 In-Home Boot Camp* is an excellent way to begin an exercise program. He follows up with *P90X*, for those who are a bit farther along. Weight Watchers and the South Beach Diet seem to have endured the test of time. I've also heard great things about *Light Weigh*, which incorporates a Catholic touch to it.

How to use the Boot Camp Journal:

1. Write your goals for the week in these spaces under the appropriate category. Remember to start slowly and grow each week.

Heart: Search & Rescue — Prayer for a specific person or intention.
Soul: Interior Life — Specifics about your own prayer life.
Mind: Spiritual Reading — Grow in understanding of your faith.
Strength: Health & Fitness — Improve and maintain your body.

2. Schedule the time of day to fulfill your goals. Write each specific action in THE DAILY PLAN section.

1   2

HEART GOALS	SOUL GOALS
Divine Mercy Chaplet for Dad	Morning Offering
	Rosary
	Examination of Conscience

MIND GOALS	STRENGTH GOALS
Prep for Total Consecration	Exercise 30 minutes

THE DAILY PLAN			
5:00 AM		1:30 PM	
5:30 AM	Morning Offering	2:00 PM	
6:00 AM	Exercise 30 minutes	2:30 PM	
6:30 AM		3:00 PM	Divine Mercy Chaplet
7:00 AM		3:30 PM	

3. Record each day how closely you followed your plan by placing a check mark in the appropriate box for each activity you completed that day. The goal is to start slowly with attainable goals and work towards filling up the grid by the end of the Boot Camp.

WEEK # 1	MON	TUE	WED	THU	FRI	SAT	SUN
HEART: SEARCH & RESCUE							
Soul in Purgatory - Indulgence							
Soul for Deeper Conversion	✓	✓		✓	✓	✓	
Day's Petitions - Pio Prayer							
SOUL: INTERIOR LIFE							
Morning Offering	✓	✓	✓	✓	✓	✓	✓
Mental Prayer							
Spiritual Reading							
Holy Mass							
Angelus (Regina Coeli)							
Holy Rosary		✓	✓		✓	✓	✓
Examination of Conscience	✓	✓	✓	✓	✓	✓	✓
MIND: SPIRITUAL READING							
Prep for Total Consecration	✓	✓	✓	✓		✓	
Catholic Lifetime Reading Plan							
Other:							
STRENGTH: HEALTH/FITNESS							
Daily Workout Goals		✓	✓	✓		✓	
Daily Dietary Goals							

CHURCH MILITANT BOOT CAMP JOURNAL

WEEKS 1 - 2 GOALS

"You shall love the Lord your God with all your heart, and with all your soul, and with all your mind, and with all your strength" (Mark 12:30).

HEART GOALS	SOUL GOALS

MIND GOALS	STRENGTH GOALS

THE DAILY PLAN

5:00 AM		1:30 PM	
5:30 AM		2:00 PM	
6:00 AM		2:30 PM	
6:30 AM		3:00 PM	
7:00 AM		3:30 PM	
7:30 AM		4:00 PM	
8:00 AM		4:30 PM	
8:30 AM		5:00 PM	
9:00 AM		5:30 PM	
9:30 AM		6:00 PM	
10:00 AM		6:30 PM	
10:30 AM		7:00 PM	
11:00 AM		7:30 PM	
11:30 AM		8:00 PM	
12:00 PM		8:30 PM	
12:30 PM		9:00 PM	
1:00 PM		9:30 PM	

WEEKS 1 – 2 PROGRESS

WEEK #__	MON	TUE	WED	THU	FRI	SAT	SUN
HEART: SEARCH & RESCUE							
Soul in Purgatory - Indulgence							
Soul for Deeper Conversion							
Day's Petitions - Pio Prayer							
SOUL: INTERIOR LIFE							
Morning Offering							
Mental Prayer							
Spiritual Reading							
Holy Mass							
Angelus (Regina Coeli)							
Holy Rosary							
Examination of Conscience							
MIND: SPIRITUAL READING							
Prep for Total Consecration							
Catholic Lifetime Reading Plan							
Other:							
STRENGTH: HEALTH/FITNESS							
Daily Workout Goals							
Daily Dietary Goals							

WEEK #__	MON	TUE	WED	THU	FRI	SAT	SUN
HEART: SEARCH & RESCUE							
Soul in Purgatory - Indulgence							
Soul for Deeper Conversion							
Day's Petitions - Pio Prayer							
SOUL: INTERIOR LIFE							
Morning Offering							
Mental Prayer							
Spiritual Reading							
Holy Mass							
Angelus (Regina Coeli)							
Holy Rosary							
Examination of Conscience							
MIND: SPIRITUAL READING							
Prep for Total Consecration							
Catholic Lifetime Reading Plan							
Other:							
STRENGTH: HEALTH/FITNESS							
Daily Workout Goals							
Daily Dietary Goals							

WEEKS 3 - 4 GOALS

"You shall love the Lord your God with all your heart, and with all your soul, and with all your mind, and with all your strength" (Mark 12:30).

HEART GOALS	SOUL GOALS

MIND GOALS	STRENGTH GOALS

THE DAILY PLAN

5:00 AM		1:30 PM	
5:30 AM		2:00 PM	
6:00 AM		2:30 PM	
6:30 AM		3:00 PM	
7:00 AM		3:30 PM	
7:30 AM		4:00 PM	
8:00 AM		4:30 PM	
8:30 AM		5:00 PM	
9:00 AM		5:30 PM	
9:30 AM		6:00 PM	
10:00 AM		6:30 PM	
10:30 AM		7:00 PM	
11:00 AM		7:30 PM	
11:30 AM		8:00 PM	
12:00 PM		8:30 PM	
12:30 PM		9:00 PM	
1:00 PM		9:30 PM	

WEEKS 3 – 4 PROGRESS

WEEK #__	MON	TUE	WED	THU	FRI	SAT	SUN
HEART: SEARCH & RESCUE							
Soul in Purgatory - Indulgence							
Soul for Deeper Conversion							
Day's Petitions - Pio Prayer							
SOUL: INTERIOR LIFE							
Morning Offering							
Mental Prayer							
Spiritual Reading							
Holy Mass							
Angelus (Regina Coeli)							
Holy Rosary							
Examination of Conscience							
MIND: SPIRITUAL READING							
Prep for Total Consecration							
Catholic Lifetime Reading Plan							
Other:							
STRENGTH: HEALTH/FITNESS							
Daily Workout Goals							
Daily Dietary Goals							

WEEK #__	MON	TUE	WED	THU	FRI	SAT	SUN
HEART: SEARCH & RESCUE							
Soul in Purgatory - Indulgence							
Soul for Deeper Conversion							
Day's Petitions - Pio Prayer							
SOUL: INTERIOR LIFE							
Morning Offering							
Mental Prayer							
Spiritual Reading							
Holy Mass							
Angelus (Regina Coeli)							
Holy Rosary							
Examination of Conscience							
MIND: SPIRITUAL READING							
Prep for Total Consecration							
Catholic Lifetime Reading Plan							
Other:							
STRENGTH: HEALTH/FITNESS							
Daily Workout Goals							
Daily Dietary Goals							

WEEKS 5 - 6 GOALS

"You shall love the Lord your God with all your heart, and with all your soul, and with all your mind, and with all your strength" (Mark 12:30).

HEART GOALS	SOUL GOALS

MIND GOALS	STRENGTH GOALS

THE DAILY PLAN

5:00 AM		1:30 PM	
5:30 AM		2:00 PM	
6:00 AM		2:30 PM	
6:30 AM		3:00 PM	
7:00 AM		3:30 PM	
7:30 AM		4:00 PM	
8:00 AM		4:30 PM	
8:30 AM		5:00 PM	
9:00 AM		5:30 PM	
9:30 AM		6:00 PM	
10:00 AM		6:30 PM	
10:30 AM		7:00 PM	
11:00 AM		7:30 PM	
11:30 AM		8:00 PM	
12:00 PM		8:30 PM	
12:30 PM		9:00 PM	
1:00 PM		9:30 PM	

WEEKS 5 – 6 PROGRESS

WEEK #__	MON	TUE	WED	THU	FRI	SAT	SUN
HEART: SEARCH & RESCUE							
Soul in Purgatory - Indulgence							
Soul for Deeper Conversion							
Day's Petitions - Pio Prayer							
SOUL: INTERIOR LIFE							
Morning Offering							
Mental Prayer							
Spiritual Reading							
Holy Mass							
Angelus (Regina Coeli)							
Holy Rosary							
Examination of Conscience							
MIND: SPIRITUAL READING							
Prep for Total Consecration							
Catholic Lifetime Reading Plan							
Other:							
STRENGTH: HEALTH/FITNESS							
Daily Workout Goals							
Daily Dietary Goals							

WEEK #__	MON	TUE	WED	THU	FRI	SAT	SUN
HEART: SEARCH & RESCUE							
Soul in Purgatory - Indulgence							
Soul for Deeper Conversion							
Day's Petitions - Pio Prayer							
SOUL: INTERIOR LIFE							
Morning Offering							
Mental Prayer							
Spiritual Reading							
Holy Mass							
Angelus (Regina Coeli)							
Holy Rosary							
Examination of Conscience							
MIND: SPIRITUAL READING							
Prep for Total Consecration							
Catholic Lifetime Reading Plan							
Other:							
STRENGTH: HEALTH/FITNESS							
Daily Workout Goals							
Daily Dietary Goals							

WEEKS 7 - 8 GOALS

"You shall love the Lord your God with all your heart, and with all your soul, and with all your mind, and with all your strength" (Mark 12:30).

HEART GOALS	SOUL GOALS

MIND GOALS	STRENGTH GOALS

THE DAILY PLAN

5:00 AM		1:30 PM	
5:30 AM		2:00 PM	
6:00 AM		2:30 PM	
6:30 AM		3:00 PM	
7:00 AM		3:30 PM	
7:30 AM		4:00 PM	
8:00 AM		4:30 PM	
8:30 AM		5:00 PM	
9:00 AM		5:30 PM	
9:30 AM		6:00 PM	
10:00 AM		6:30 PM	
10:30 AM		7:00 PM	
11:00 AM		7:30 PM	
11:30 AM		8:00 PM	
12:00 PM		8:30 PM	
12:30 PM		9:00 PM	
1:00 PM		9:30 PM	

WEEKS 7 – 8 PROGRESS

WEEK #__	MON	TUE	WED	THU	FRI	SAT	SUN
HEART: SEARCH & RESCUE							
Soul in Purgatory - Indulgence							
Soul for Deeper Conversion							
Day's Petitions - Pio Prayer							
SOUL: INTERIOR LIFE							
Morning Offering							
Mental Prayer							
Spiritual Reading							
Holy Mass							
Angelus (Regina Coeli)							
Holy Rosary							
Examination of Conscience							
MIND: SPIRITUAL READING							
Prep for Total Consecration							
Catholic Lifetime Reading Plan							
Other:							
STRENGTH: HEALTH/FITNESS							
Daily Workout Goals							
Daily Dietary Goals							

WEEK #__	MON	TUE	WED	THU	FRI	SAT	SUN
HEART: SEARCH & RESCUE							
Soul in Purgatory - Indulgence							
Soul for Deeper Conversion							
Day's Petitions - Pio Prayer							
SOUL: INTERIOR LIFE							
Morning Offering							
Mental Prayer							
Spiritual Reading							
Holy Mass							
Angelus (Regina Coeli)							
Holy Rosary							
Examination of Conscience							
MIND: SPIRITUAL READING							
Prep for Total Consecration							
Catholic Lifetime Reading Plan							
Other:							
STRENGTH: HEALTH/FITNESS							
Daily Workout Goals							
Daily Dietary Goals							

WEEKS 9 - 10 GOALS

"You shall love the Lord your God with all your heart, and with all your soul, and with all your mind, and with all your strength" (Mark 12:30).

HEART GOALS	SOUL GOALS

MIND GOALS	STRENGTH GOALS

THE DAILY PLAN

5:00 AM		1:30 PM	
5:30 AM		2:00 PM	
6:00 AM		2:30 PM	
6:30 AM		3:00 PM	
7:00 AM		3:30 PM	
7:30 AM		4:00 PM	
8:00 AM		4:30 PM	
8:30 AM		5:00 PM	
9:00 AM		5:30 PM	
9:30 AM		6:00 PM	
10:00 AM		6:30 PM	
10:30 AM		7:00 PM	
11:00 AM		7:30 PM	
11:30 AM		8:00 PM	
12:00 PM		8:30 PM	
12:30 PM		9:00 PM	
1:00 PM		9:30 PM	

WEEKS 9 – 10 PROGRESS

WEEK #__	MON	TUE	WED	THU	FRI	SAT	SUN
HEART: SEARCH & RESCUE							
Soul in Purgatory - Indulgence							
Soul for Deeper Conversion							
Day's Petitions - Pio Prayer							
SOUL: INTERIOR LIFE							
Morning Offering							
Mental Prayer							
Spiritual Reading							
Holy Mass							
Angelus (Regina Coeli)							
Holy Rosary							
Examination of Conscience							
MIND: SPIRITUAL READING							
Prep for Total Consecration							
Catholic Lifetime Reading Plan							
Other:							
STRENGTH: HEALTH/FITNESS							
Daily Workout Goals							
Daily Dietary Goals							

WEEK #__	MON	TUE	WED	THU	FRI	SAT	SUN
HEART: SEARCH & RESCUE							
Soul in Purgatory - Indulgence							
Soul for Deeper Conversion							
Day's Petitions - Pio Prayer							
SOUL: INTERIOR LIFE							
Morning Offering							
Mental Prayer							
Spiritual Reading							
Holy Mass							
Angelus (Regina Coeli)							
Holy Rosary							
Examination of Conscience							
MIND: SPIRITUAL READING							
Prep for Total Consecration							
Catholic Lifetime Reading Plan							
Other:							
STRENGTH: HEALTH/FITNESS							
Daily Workout Goals							
Daily Dietary Goals							

WEEKS 11 - 12 GOALS

"You shall love the Lord your God with all your heart, and with all your soul, and with all your mind, and with all your strength" (Mark 12:30).

HEART GOALS	SOUL GOALS

MIND GOALS	STRENGTH GOALS

THE DAILY PLAN			
5:00 AM		1:30 PM	
5:30 AM		2:00 PM	
6:00 AM		2:30 PM	
6:30 AM		3:00 PM	
7:00 AM		3:30 PM	
7:30 AM		4:00 PM	
8:00 AM		4:30 PM	
8:30 AM		5:00 PM	
9:00 AM		5:30 PM	
9:30 AM		6:00 PM	
10:00 AM		6:30 PM	
10:30 AM		7:00 PM	
11:00 AM		7:30 PM	
11:30 AM		8:00 PM	
12:00 PM		8:30 PM	
12:30 PM		9:00 PM	
1:00 PM		9:30 PM	

WEEKS 11 – 12 PROGRESS

WEEK #__	MON	TUE	WED	THU	FRI	SAT	SUN
HEART: SEARCH & RESCUE							
Soul in Purgatory - Indulgence							
Soul for Deeper Conversion							
Day's Petitions - Pio Prayer							
SOUL: INTERIOR LIFE							
Morning Offering							
Mental Prayer							
Spiritual Reading							
Holy Mass							
Angelus (Regina Coeli)							
Holy Rosary							
Examination of Conscience							
MIND: SPIRITUAL READING							
Prep for Total Consecration							
Catholic Lifetime Reading Plan							
Other:							
STRENGTH: HEALTH/FITNESS							
Daily Workout Goals							
Daily Dietary Goals							

WEEK #__	MON	TUE	WED	THU	FRI	SAT	SUN
HEART: SEARCH & RESCUE							
Soul in Purgatory - Indulgence							
Soul for Deeper Conversion							
Day's Petitions - Pio Prayer							
SOUL: INTERIOR LIFE							
Morning Offering							
Mental Prayer							
Spiritual Reading							
Holy Mass							
Angelus (Regina Coeli)							
Holy Rosary							
Examination of Conscience							
MIND: SPIRITUAL READING							
Prep for Total Consecration							
Catholic Lifetime Reading Plan							
Other:							
STRENGTH: HEALTH/FITNESS							
Daily Workout Goals							
Daily Dietary Goals							

WEEKS 13 - 14 GOALS

"You shall love the Lord your God with all your heart, and with all your soul, and with all your mind, and with all your strength" (Mark 12:30).

HEART GOALS	SOUL GOALS

MIND GOALS	STRENGTH GOALS

THE DAILY PLAN

5:00 AM		1:30 PM	
5:30 AM		2:00 PM	
6:00 AM		2:30 PM	
6:30 AM		3:00 PM	
7:00 AM		3:30 PM	
7:30 AM		4:00 PM	
8:00 AM		4:30 PM	
8:30 AM		5:00 PM	
9:00 AM		5:30 PM	
9:30 AM		6:00 PM	
10:00 AM		6:30 PM	
10:30 AM		7:00 PM	
11:00 AM		7:30 PM	
11:30 AM		8:00 PM	
12:00 PM		8:30 PM	
12:30 PM		9:00 PM	
1:00 PM		9:30 PM	

WEEKS 13 – 14 PROGRESS

WEEK #__	MON	TUE	WED	THU	FRI	SAT	SUN
HEART: SEARCH & RESCUE							
Soul in Purgatory - Indulgence							
Soul for Deeper Conversion							
Day's Petitions - Pio Prayer							
SOUL: INTERIOR LIFE							
Morning Offering							
Mental Prayer							
Spiritual Reading							
Holy Mass							
Angelus (Regina Coeli)							
Holy Rosary							
Examination of Conscience							
MIND: SPIRITUAL READING							
Prep for Total Consecration							
Catholic Lifetime Reading Plan							
Other:							
STRENGTH: HEALTH/FITNESS							
Daily Workout Goals							
Daily Dietary Goals							

WEEK #__	MON	TUE	WED	THU	FRI	SAT	SUN
HEART: SEARCH & RESCUE							
Soul in Purgatory - Indulgence							
Soul for Deeper Conversion							
Day's Petitions - Pio Prayer							
SOUL: INTERIOR LIFE							
Morning Offering							
Mental Prayer							
Spiritual Reading							
Holy Mass							
Angelus (Regina Coeli)							
Holy Rosary							
Examination of Conscience							
MIND: SPIRITUAL READING							
Prep for Total Consecration							
Catholic Lifetime Reading Plan							
Other:							
STRENGTH: HEALTH/FITNESS							
Daily Workout Goals							
Daily Dietary Goals							

WEEKS 15 - 16 GOALS

"You shall love the Lord your God with all your heart, and with all your soul, and with all your mind, and with all your strength" (Mark 12:30).

HEART GOALS	SOUL GOALS

MIND GOALS	STRENGTH GOALS

THE DAILY PLAN

5:00 AM		1:30 PM	
5:30 AM		2:00 PM	
6:00 AM		2:30 PM	
6:30 AM		3:00 PM	
7:00 AM		3:30 PM	
7:30 AM		4:00 PM	
8:00 AM		4:30 PM	
8:30 AM		5:00 PM	
9:00 AM		5:30 PM	
9:30 AM		6:00 PM	
10:00 AM		6:30 PM	
10:30 AM		7:00 PM	
11:00 AM		7:30 PM	
11:30 AM		8:00 PM	
12:00 PM		8:30 PM	
12:30 PM		9:00 PM	
1:00 PM		9:30 PM	

WEEKS 15 – 16 PROGRESS

WEEK #__	MON	TUE	WED	THU	FRI	SAT	SUN
HEART: SEARCH & RESCUE							
Soul in Purgatory - Indulgence							
Soul for Deeper Conversion							
Day's Petitions - Pio Prayer							
SOUL: INTERIOR LIFE							
Morning Offering							
Mental Prayer							
Spiritual Reading							
Holy Mass							
Angelus (Regina Coeli)							
Holy Rosary							
Examination of Conscience							
MIND: SPIRITUAL READING							
Prep for Total Consecration							
Catholic Lifetime Reading Plan							
Other:							
STRENGTH: HEALTH/FITNESS							
Daily Workout Goals							
Daily Dietary Goals							

WEEK #__	MON	TUE	WED	THU	FRI	SAT	SUN
HEART: SEARCH & RESCUE							
Soul in Purgatory - Indulgence							
Soul for Deeper Conversion							
Day's Petitions - Pio Prayer							
SOUL: INTERIOR LIFE							
Morning Offering							
Mental Prayer							
Spiritual Reading							
Holy Mass							
Angelus (Regina Coeli)							
Holy Rosary							
Examination of Conscience							
MIND: SPIRITUAL READING							
Prep for Total Consecration							
Catholic Lifetime Reading Plan							
Other:							
STRENGTH: HEALTH/FITNESS							
Daily Workout Goals							
Daily Dietary Goals							

WEEKS 17 - 18 GOALS

"You shall love the Lord your God with all your heart, and with all your soul, and with all your mind, and with all your strength" (Mark 12:30).

HEART GOALS	SOUL GOALS

MIND GOALS	STRENGTH GOALS

THE DAILY PLAN

5:00 AM		1:30 PM	
5:30 AM		2:00 PM	
6:00 AM		2:30 PM	
6:30 AM		3:00 PM	
7:00 AM		3:30 PM	
7:30 AM		4:00 PM	
8:00 AM		4:30 PM	
8:30 AM		5:00 PM	
9:00 AM		5:30 PM	
9:30 AM		6:00 PM	
10:00 AM		6:30 PM	
10:30 AM		7:00 PM	
11:00 AM		7:30 PM	
11:30 AM		8:00 PM	
12:00 PM		8:30 PM	
12:30 PM		9:00 PM	
1:00 PM		9:30 PM	

WEEKS 17 – 18 PROGRESS

WEEK #__	MON	TUE	WED	THU	FRI	SAT	SUN
HEART: SEARCH & RESCUE							
Soul in Purgatory - Indulgence							
Soul for Deeper Conversion							
Day's Petitions - Pio Prayer							
SOUL: INTERIOR LIFE							
Morning Offering							
Mental Prayer							
Spiritual Reading							
Holy Mass							
Angelus (Regina Coeli)							
Holy Rosary							
Examination of Conscience							
MIND: SPIRITUAL READING							
Prep for Total Consecration							
Catholic Lifetime Reading Plan							
Other:							
STRENGTH: HEALTH/FITNESS							
Daily Workout Goals							
Daily Dietary Goals							

WEEK #__	MON	TUE	WED	THU	FRI	SAT	SUN
HEART: SEARCH & RESCUE							
Soul in Purgatory - Indulgence							
Soul for Deeper Conversion							
Day's Petitions - Pio Prayer							
SOUL: INTERIOR LIFE							
Morning Offering							
Mental Prayer							
Spiritual Reading							
Holy Mass							
Angelus (Regina Coeli)							
Holy Rosary							
Examination of Conscience							
MIND: SPIRITUAL READING							
Prep for Total Consecration							
Catholic Lifetime Reading Plan							
Other:							
STRENGTH: HEALTH/FITNESS							
Daily Workout Goals							
Daily Dietary Goals							

WEEKS 19 - 20 GOALS

"You shall love the Lord your God with all your heart, and with all your soul, and with all your mind, and with all your strength" (Mark 12:30).

HEART GOALS	SOUL GOALS

MIND GOALS	STRENGTH GOALS

THE DAILY PLAN

5:00 AM		1:30 PM	
5:30 AM		2:00 PM	
6:00 AM		2:30 PM	
6:30 AM		3:00 PM	
7:00 AM		3:30 PM	
7:30 AM		4:00 PM	
8:00 AM		4:30 PM	
8:30 AM		5:00 PM	
9:00 AM		5:30 PM	
9:30 AM		6:00 PM	
10:00 AM		6:30 PM	
10:30 AM		7:00 PM	
11:00 AM		7:30 PM	
11:30 AM		8:00 PM	
12:00 PM		8:30 PM	
12:30 PM		9:00 PM	
1:00 PM		9:30 PM	

WEEKS 19 – 20 PROGRESS

WEEK #__	MON	TUE	WED	THU	FRI	SAT	SUN
HEART: SEARCH & RESCUE							
Soul in Purgatory - Indulgence							
Soul for Deeper Conversion							
Day's Petitions - Pio Prayer							
SOUL: INTERIOR LIFE							
Morning Offering							
Mental Prayer							
Spiritual Reading							
Holy Mass							
Angelus (Regina Coeli)							
Holy Rosary							
Examination of Conscience							
MIND: SPIRITUAL READING							
Prep for Total Consecration							
Catholic Lifetime Reading Plan							
Other:							
STRENGTH: HEALTH/FITNESS							
Daily Workout Goals							
Daily Dietary Goals							

WEEK #__	MON	TUE	WED	THU	FRI	SAT	SUN
HEART: SEARCH & RESCUE							
Soul in Purgatory - Indulgence							
Soul for Deeper Conversion							
Day's Petitions - Pio Prayer							
SOUL: INTERIOR LIFE							
Morning Offering							
Mental Prayer							
Spiritual Reading							
Holy Mass							
Angelus (Regina Coeli)							
Holy Rosary							
Examination of Conscience							
MIND: SPIRITUAL READING							
Prep for Total Consecration							
Catholic Lifetime Reading Plan							
Other:							
STRENGTH: HEALTH/FITNESS							
Daily Workout Goals							
Daily Dietary Goals							

WEEKS 21 - 22 GOALS

"You shall love the Lord your God with all your heart, and with all your soul, and with all your mind, and with all your strength" (Mark 12:30).

HEART GOALS	SOUL GOALS

MIND GOALS	STRENGTH GOALS

THE DAILY PLAN

5:00 AM		1:30 PM	
5:30 AM		2:00 PM	
6:00 AM		2:30 PM	
6:30 AM		3:00 PM	
7:00 AM		3:30 PM	
7:30 AM		4:00 PM	
8:00 AM		4:30 PM	
8:30 AM		5:00 PM	
9:00 AM		5:30 PM	
9:30 AM		6:00 PM	
10:00 AM		6:30 PM	
10:30 AM		7:00 PM	
11:00 AM		7:30 PM	
11:30 AM		8:00 PM	
12:00 PM		8:30 PM	
12:30 PM		9:00 PM	
1:00 PM		9:30 PM	

WEEKS 21 – 22 PROGRESS

WEEK #__	MON	TUE	WED	THU	FRI	SAT	SUN
HEART: SEARCH & RESCUE							
Soul in Purgatory - Indulgence							
Soul for Deeper Conversion							
Day's Petitions - Pio Prayer							
SOUL: INTERIOR LIFE							
Morning Offering							
Mental Prayer							
Spiritual Reading							
Holy Mass							
Angelus (Regina Coeli)							
Holy Rosary							
Examination of Conscience							
MIND: SPIRITUAL READING							
Prep for Total Consecration							
Catholic Lifetime Reading Plan							
Other:							
STRENGTH: HEALTH/FITNESS							
Daily Workout Goals							
Daily Dietary Goals							

WEEK #__	MON	TUE	WED	THU	FRI	SAT	SUN
HEART: SEARCH & RESCUE							
Soul in Purgatory - Indulgence							
Soul for Deeper Conversion							
Day's Petitions - Pio Prayer							
SOUL: INTERIOR LIFE							
Morning Offering							
Mental Prayer							
Spiritual Reading							
Holy Mass							
Angelus (Regina Coeli)							
Holy Rosary							
Examination of Conscience							
MIND: SPIRITUAL READING							
Prep for Total Consecration							
Catholic Lifetime Reading Plan							
Other:							
STRENGTH: HEALTH/FITNESS							
Daily Workout Goals							
Daily Dietary Goals							

WEEKS 23 - 24 GOALS

"You shall love the Lord your God with all your heart, and with all your soul, and with all your mind, and with all your strength" (Mark 12:30).

HEART GOALS	SOUL GOALS

MIND GOALS	STRENGTH GOALS

THE DAILY PLAN

5:00 AM		1:30 PM	
5:30 AM		2:00 PM	
6:00 AM		2:30 PM	
6:30 AM		3:00 PM	
7:00 AM		3:30 PM	
7:30 AM		4:00 PM	
8:00 AM		4:30 PM	
8:30 AM		5:00 PM	
9:00 AM		5:30 PM	
9:30 AM		6:00 PM	
10:00 AM		6:30 PM	
10:30 AM		7:00 PM	
11:00 AM		7:30 PM	
11:30 AM		8:00 PM	
12:00 PM		8:30 PM	
12:30 PM		9:00 PM	
1:00 PM		9:30 PM	

WEEKS 23 – 24 PROGRESS

WEEK #__	MON	TUE	WED	THU	FRI	SAT	SUN
HEART: SEARCH & RESCUE							
Soul in Purgatory - Indulgence							
Soul for Deeper Conversion							
Day's Petitions - Pio Prayer							
SOUL: INTERIOR LIFE							
Morning Offering							
Mental Prayer							
Spiritual Reading							
Holy Mass							
Angelus (Regina Coeli)							
Holy Rosary							
Examination of Conscience							
MIND: SPIRITUAL READING							
Prep for Total Consecration							
Catholic Lifetime Reading Plan							
Other:							
STRENGTH: HEALTH/FITNESS							
Daily Workout Goals							
Daily Dietary Goals							

WEEK #__	MON	TUE	WED	THU	FRI	SAT	SUN
HEART: SEARCH & RESCUE							
Soul in Purgatory - Indulgence							
Soul for Deeper Conversion							
Day's Petitions - Pio Prayer							
SOUL: INTERIOR LIFE							
Morning Offering							
Mental Prayer							
Spiritual Reading							
Holy Mass							
Angelus (Regina Coeli)							
Holy Rosary							
Examination of Conscience							
MIND: SPIRITUAL READING							
Prep for Total Consecration							
Catholic Lifetime Reading Plan							
Other:							
STRENGTH: HEALTH/FITNESS							
Daily Workout Goals							
Daily Dietary Goals							

WEEKS 25 - 26 GOALS

"You shall love the Lord your God with all your heart, and with all your soul, and with all your mind, and with all your strength" (Mark 12:30).

HEART GOALS	SOUL GOALS

MIND GOALS	STRENGTH GOALS

THE DAILY PLAN

5:00 AM		1:30 PM	
5:30 AM		2:00 PM	
6:00 AM		2:30 PM	
6:30 AM		3:00 PM	
7:00 AM		3:30 PM	
7:30 AM		4:00 PM	
8:00 AM		4:30 PM	
8:30 AM		5:00 PM	
9:00 AM		5:30 PM	
9:30 AM		6:00 PM	
10:00 AM		6:30 PM	
10:30 AM		7:00 PM	
11:00 AM		7:30 PM	
11:30 AM		8:00 PM	
12:00 PM		8:30 PM	
12:30 PM		9:00 PM	
1:00 PM		9:30 PM	

WEEKS 25 – 26 PROGRESS

WEEK #__	MON	TUE	WED	THU	FRI	SAT	SUN
HEART: SEARCH & RESCUE							
Soul in Purgatory - Indulgence							
Soul for Deeper Conversion							
Day's Petitions - Pio Prayer							
SOUL: INTERIOR LIFE							
Morning Offering							
Mental Prayer							
Spiritual Reading							
Holy Mass							
Angelus (Regina Coeli)							
Holy Rosary							
Examination of Conscience							
MIND: SPIRITUAL READING							
Prep for Total Consecration							
Catholic Lifetime Reading Plan							
Other:							
STRENGTH: HEALTH/FITNESS							
Daily Workout Goals							
Daily Dietary Goals							

WEEK #__	MON	TUE	WED	THU	FRI	SAT	SUN
HEART: SEARCH & RESCUE							
Soul in Purgatory - Indulgence							
Soul for Deeper Conversion							
Day's Petitions - Pio Prayer							
SOUL: INTERIOR LIFE							
Morning Offering							
Mental Prayer							
Spiritual Reading							
Holy Mass							
Angelus (Regina Coeli)							
Holy Rosary							
Examination of Conscience							
MIND: SPIRITUAL READING							
Prep for Total Consecration							
Catholic Lifetime Reading Plan							
Other:							
STRENGTH: HEALTH/FITNESS							
Daily Workout Goals							
Daily Dietary Goals							

WEEKS 27 - 28 GOALS

"You shall love the Lord your God with all your heart, and with all your soul, and with all your mind, and with all your strength" (Mark 12:30).

HEART GOALS	SOUL GOALS

MIND GOALS	STRENGTH GOALS

THE DAILY PLAN

5:00 AM		1:30 PM	
5:30 AM		2:00 PM	
6:00 AM		2:30 PM	
6:30 AM		3:00 PM	
7:00 AM		3:30 PM	
7:30 AM		4:00 PM	
8:00 AM		4:30 PM	
8:30 AM		5:00 PM	
9:00 AM		5:30 PM	
9:30 AM		6:00 PM	
10:00 AM		6:30 PM	
10:30 AM		7:00 PM	
11:00 AM		7:30 PM	
11:30 AM		8:00 PM	
12:00 PM		8:30 PM	
12:30 PM		9:00 PM	
1:00 PM		9:30 PM	

WEEKS 27 – 28 PROGRESS

WEEK #__	MON	TUE	WED	THU	FRI	SAT	SUN
HEART: SEARCH & RESCUE							
Soul in Purgatory - Indulgence							
Soul for Deeper Conversion							
Day's Petitions - Pio Prayer							
SOUL: INTERIOR LIFE							
Morning Offering							
Mental Prayer							
Spiritual Reading							
Holy Mass							
Angelus (Regina Coeli)							
Holy Rosary							
Examination of Conscience							
MIND: SPIRITUAL READING							
Prep for Total Consecration							
Catholic Lifetime Reading Plan							
Other:							
STRENGTH: HEALTH/FITNESS							
Daily Workout Goals							
Daily Dietary Goals							

WEEK #__	MON	TUE	WED	THU	FRI	SAT	SUN
HEART: SEARCH & RESCUE							
Soul in Purgatory - Indulgence							
Soul for Deeper Conversion							
Day's Petitions - Pio Prayer							
SOUL: INTERIOR LIFE							
Morning Offering							
Mental Prayer							
Spiritual Reading							
Holy Mass							
Angelus (Regina Coeli)							
Holy Rosary							
Examination of Conscience							
MIND: SPIRITUAL READING							
Prep for Total Consecration							
Catholic Lifetime Reading Plan							
Other:							
STRENGTH: HEALTH/FITNESS							
Daily Workout Goals							
Daily Dietary Goals							

WEEKS 29 - 30 GOALS

"You shall love the Lord your God with all your heart, and with all your soul, and with all your mind, and with all your strength" (Mark 12:30).

HEART GOALS	SOUL GOALS

MIND GOALS	STRENGTH GOALS

THE DAILY PLAN			
5:00 AM		1:30 PM	
5:30 AM		2:00 PM	
6:00 AM		2:30 PM	
6:30 AM		3:00 PM	
7:00 AM		3:30 PM	
7:30 AM		4:00 PM	
8:00 AM		4:30 PM	
8:30 AM		5:00 PM	
9:00 AM		5:30 PM	
9:30 AM		6:00 PM	
10:00 AM		6:30 PM	
10:30 AM		7:00 PM	
11:00 AM		7:30 PM	
11:30 AM		8:00 PM	
12:00 PM		8:30 PM	
12:30 PM		9:00 PM	
1:00 PM		9:30 PM	

152

WEEKS 29 – 30 PROGRESS

WEEK #__	MON	TUE	WED	THU	FRI	SAT	SUN
HEART: SEARCH & RESCUE							
Soul in Purgatory - Indulgence							
Soul for Deeper Conversion							
Day's Petitions - Pio Prayer							
SOUL: INTERIOR LIFE							
Morning Offering							
Mental Prayer							
Spiritual Reading							
Holy Mass							
Angelus (Regina Coeli)							
Holy Rosary							
Examination of Conscience							
MIND: SPIRITUAL READING							
Prep for Total Consecration							
Catholic Lifetime Reading Plan							
Other:							
STRENGTH: HEALTH/FITNESS							
Daily Workout Goals							
Daily Dietary Goals							

WEEK #__	MON	TUE	WED	THU	FRI	SAT	SUN
HEART: SEARCH & RESCUE							
Soul in Purgatory - Indulgence							
Soul for Deeper Conversion							
Day's Petitions - Pio Prayer							
SOUL: INTERIOR LIFE							
Morning Offering							
Mental Prayer							
Spiritual Reading							
Holy Mass							
Angelus (Regina Coeli)							
Holy Rosary							
Examination of Conscience							
MIND: SPIRITUAL READING							
Prep for Total Consecration							
Catholic Lifetime Reading Plan							
Other:							
STRENGTH: HEALTH/FITNESS							
Daily Workout Goals							
Daily Dietary Goals							

WEEKS 31 - 32 GOALS

"You shall love the Lord your God with all your heart, and with all your soul, and with all your mind, and with all your strength" (Mark 12:30).

HEART GOALS	SOUL GOALS

MIND GOALS	STRENGTH GOALS

THE DAILY PLAN

5:00 AM		1:30 PM	
5:30 AM		2:00 PM	
6:00 AM		2:30 PM	
6:30 AM		3:00 PM	
7:00 AM		3:30 PM	
7:30 AM		4:00 PM	
8:00 AM		4:30 PM	
8:30 AM		5:00 PM	
9:00 AM		5:30 PM	
9:30 AM		6:00 PM	
10:00 AM		6:30 PM	
10:30 AM		7:00 PM	
11:00 AM		7:30 PM	
11:30 AM		8:00 PM	
12:00 PM		8:30 PM	
12:30 PM		9:00 PM	
1:00 PM		9:30 PM	

154

WEEKS 31 – 32 PROGRESS

WEEK #__	MON	TUE	WED	THU	FRI	SAT	SUN
HEART: SEARCH & RESCUE							
Soul in Purgatory - Indulgence							
Soul for Deeper Conversion							
Day's Petitions - Pio Prayer							
SOUL: INTERIOR LIFE							
Morning Offering							
Mental Prayer							
Spiritual Reading							
Holy Mass							
Angelus (Regina Coeli)							
Holy Rosary							
Examination of Conscience							
MIND: SPIRITUAL READING							
Prep for Total Consecration							
Catholic Lifetime Reading Plan							
Other:							
STRENGTH: HEALTH/FITNESS							
Daily Workout Goals							
Daily Dietary Goals							

WEEK #__	MON	TUE	WED	THU	FRI	SAT	SUN
HEART: SEARCH & RESCUE							
Soul in Purgatory - Indulgence							
Soul for Deeper Conversion							
Day's Petitions - Pio Prayer							
SOUL: INTERIOR LIFE							
Morning Offering							
Mental Prayer							
Spiritual Reading							
Holy Mass							
Angelus (Regina Coeli)							
Holy Rosary							
Examination of Conscience							
MIND: SPIRITUAL READING							
Prep for Total Consecration							
Catholic Lifetime Reading Plan							
Other:							
STRENGTH: HEALTH/FITNESS							
Daily Workout Goals							
Daily Dietary Goals							

WEEKS 33 - 34 GOALS

"You shall love the Lord your God with all your heart, and with all your soul, and with all your mind, and with all your strength" (Mark 12:30).

HEART GOALS	SOUL GOALS

MIND GOALS	STRENGTH GOALS

THE DAILY PLAN

5:00 AM		1:30 PM	
5:30 AM		2:00 PM	
6:00 AM		2:30 PM	
6:30 AM		3:00 PM	
7:00 AM		3:30 PM	
7:30 AM		4:00 PM	
8:00 AM		4:30 PM	
8:30 AM		5:00 PM	
9:00 AM		5:30 PM	
9:30 AM		6:00 PM	
10:00 AM		6:30 PM	
10:30 AM		7:00 PM	
11:00 AM		7:30 PM	
11:30 AM		8:00 PM	
12:00 PM		8:30 PM	
12:30 PM		9:00 PM	
1:00 PM		9:30 PM	

WEEKS 33 – 34 PROGRESS

WEEK #__	MON	TUE	WED	THU	FRI	SAT	SUN
HEART: SEARCH & RESCUE							
Soul in Purgatory - Indulgence							
Soul for Deeper Conversion							
Day's Petitions - Pio Prayer							
SOUL: INTERIOR LIFE							
Morning Offering							
Mental Prayer							
Spiritual Reading							
Holy Mass							
Angelus (Regina Coeli)							
Holy Rosary							
Examination of Conscience							
MIND: SPIRITUAL READING							
Prep for Total Consecration							
Catholic Lifetime Reading Plan							
Other:							
STRENGTH: HEALTH/FITNESS							
Daily Workout Goals							
Daily Dietary Goals							

WEEK #__	MON	TUE	WED	THU	FRI	SAT	SUN
HEART: SEARCH & RESCUE							
Soul in Purgatory - Indulgence							
Soul for Deeper Conversion							
Day's Petitions - Pio Prayer							
SOUL: INTERIOR LIFE							
Morning Offering							
Mental Prayer							
Spiritual Reading							
Holy Mass							
Angelus (Regina Coeli)							
Holy Rosary							
Examination of Conscience							
MIND: SPIRITUAL READING							
Prep for Total Consecration							
Catholic Lifetime Reading Plan							
Other:							
STRENGTH: HEALTH/FITNESS							
Daily Workout Goals							
Daily Dietary Goals							

WEEKS 35 - 36 GOALS

"You shall love the Lord your God with all your heart, and with all your soul, and with all your mind, and with all your strength" (Mark 12:30).

HEART GOALS	SOUL GOALS

MIND GOALS	STRENGTH GOALS

THE DAILY PLAN

5:00 AM		1:30 PM	
5:30 AM		2:00 PM	
6:00 AM		2:30 PM	
6:30 AM		3:00 PM	
7:00 AM		3:30 PM	
7:30 AM		4:00 PM	
8:00 AM		4:30 PM	
8:30 AM		5:00 PM	
9:00 AM		5:30 PM	
9:30 AM		6:00 PM	
10:00 AM		6:30 PM	
10:30 AM		7:00 PM	
11:00 AM		7:30 PM	
11:30 AM		8:00 PM	
12:00 PM		8:30 PM	
12:30 PM		9:00 PM	
1:00 PM		9:30 PM	

WEEKS 35 – 36 PROGRESS

WEEK #__	MON	TUE	WED	THU	FRI	SAT	SUN
HEART: SEARCH & RESCUE							
Soul in Purgatory - Indulgence							
Soul for Deeper Conversion							
Day's Petitions - Pio Prayer							
SOUL: INTERIOR LIFE							
Morning Offering							
Mental Prayer							
Spiritual Reading							
Holy Mass							
Angelus (Regina Coeli)							
Holy Rosary							
Examination of Conscience							
MIND: SPIRITUAL READING							
Prep for Total Consecration							
Catholic Lifetime Reading Plan							
Other:							
STRENGTH: HEALTH/FITNESS							
Daily Workout Goals							
Daily Dietary Goals							

WEEK #__	MON	TUE	WED	THU	FRI	SAT	SUN
HEART: SEARCH & RESCUE							
Soul in Purgatory - Indulgence							
Soul for Deeper Conversion							
Day's Petitions - Pio Prayer							
SOUL: INTERIOR LIFE							
Morning Offering							
Mental Prayer							
Spiritual Reading							
Holy Mass							
Angelus (Regina Coeli)							
Holy Rosary							
Examination of Conscience							
MIND: SPIRITUAL READING							
Prep for Total Consecration							
Catholic Lifetime Reading Plan							
Other:							
STRENGTH: HEALTH/FITNESS							
Daily Workout Goals							
Daily Dietary Goals							

WEEKS 37 - 38 GOALS

"You shall love the Lord your God with all your heart, and with all your soul, and with all your mind, and with all your strength" (Mark 12:30).

HEART GOALS	SOUL GOALS

MIND GOALS	STRENGTH GOALS

THE DAILY PLAN			
5:00 AM		1:30 PM	
5:30 AM		2:00 PM	
6:00 AM		2:30 PM	
6:30 AM		3:00 PM	
7:00 AM		3:30 PM	
7:30 AM		4:00 PM	
8:00 AM		4:30 PM	
8:30 AM		5:00 PM	
9:00 AM		5:30 PM	
9:30 AM		6:00 PM	
10:00 AM		6:30 PM	
10:30 AM		7:00 PM	
11:00 AM		7:30 PM	
11:30 AM		8:00 PM	
12:00 PM		8:30 PM	
12:30 PM		9:00 PM	
1:00 PM		9:30 PM	

WEEKS 37 – 38 PROGRESS

WEEK #__	MON	TUE	WED	THU	FRI	SAT	SUN
HEART: SEARCH & RESCUE							
Soul in Purgatory - Indulgence							
Soul for Deeper Conversion							
Day's Petitions - Pio Prayer							
SOUL: INTERIOR LIFE							
Morning Offering							
Mental Prayer							
Spiritual Reading							
Holy Mass							
Angelus (Regina Coeli)							
Holy Rosary							
Examination of Conscience							
MIND: SPIRITUAL READING							
Prep for Total Consecration							
Catholic Lifetime Reading Plan							
Other:							
STRENGTH: HEALTH/FITNESS							
Daily Workout Goals							
Daily Dietary Goals							

WEEK #__	MON	TUE	WED	THU	FRI	SAT	SUN
HEART: SEARCH & RESCUE							
Soul in Purgatory - Indulgence							
Soul for Deeper Conversion							
Day's Petitions - Pio Prayer							
SOUL: INTERIOR LIFE							
Morning Offering							
Mental Prayer							
Spiritual Reading							
Holy Mass							
Angelus (Regina Coeli)							
Holy Rosary							
Examination of Conscience							
MIND: SPIRITUAL READING							
Prep for Total Consecration							
Catholic Lifetime Reading Plan							
Other:							
STRENGTH: HEALTH/FITNESS							
Daily Workout Goals							
Daily Dietary Goals							

WEEKS 39 - 40 GOALS

"You shall love the Lord your God with all your heart, and with all your soul, and with all your mind, and with all your strength" (Mark 12:30).

HEART GOALS	SOUL GOALS

MIND GOALS	STRENGTH GOALS

THE DAILY PLAN

5:00 AM		1:30 PM	
5:30 AM		2:00 PM	
6:00 AM		2:30 PM	
6:30 AM		3:00 PM	
7:00 AM		3:30 PM	
7:30 AM		4:00 PM	
8:00 AM		4:30 PM	
8:30 AM		5:00 PM	
9:00 AM		5:30 PM	
9:30 AM		6:00 PM	
10:00 AM		6:30 PM	
10:30 AM		7:00 PM	
11:00 AM		7:30 PM	
11:30 AM		8:00 PM	
12:00 PM		8:30 PM	
12:30 PM		9:00 PM	
1:00 PM		9:30 PM	

WEEKS 39 – 40 PROGRESS

WEEK #__	MON	TUE	WED	THU	FRI	SAT	SUN
HEART: SEARCH & RESCUE							
Soul in Purgatory - Indulgence							
Soul for Deeper Conversion							
Day's Petitions - Pio Prayer							
SOUL: INTERIOR LIFE							
Morning Offering							
Mental Prayer							
Spiritual Reading							
Holy Mass							
Angelus (Regina Coeli)							
Holy Rosary							
Examination of Conscience							
MIND: SPIRITUAL READING							
Prep for Total Consecration							
Catholic Lifetime Reading Plan							
Other:							
STRENGTH: HEALTH/FITNESS							
Daily Workout Goals							
Daily Dietary Goals							

WEEK #__	MON	TUE	WED	THU	FRI	SAT	SUN
HEART: SEARCH & RESCUE							
Soul in Purgatory - Indulgence							
Soul for Deeper Conversion							
Day's Petitions - Pio Prayer							
SOUL: INTERIOR LIFE							
Morning Offering							
Mental Prayer							
Spiritual Reading							
Holy Mass							
Angelus (Regina Coeli)							
Holy Rosary							
Examination of Conscience							
MIND: SPIRITUAL READING							
Prep for Total Consecration							
Catholic Lifetime Reading Plan							
Other:							
STRENGTH: HEALTH/FITNESS							
Daily Workout Goals							
Daily Dietary Goals							

WEEKS 41 - 42 GOALS

"You shall love the Lord your God with all your heart, and with all your soul, and with all your mind, and with all your strength" (Mark 12:30).

HEART GOALS	SOUL GOALS

MIND GOALS	STRENGTH GOALS

THE DAILY PLAN

5:00 AM		1:30 PM	
5:30 AM		2:00 PM	
6:00 AM		2:30 PM	
6:30 AM		3:00 PM	
7:00 AM		3:30 PM	
7:30 AM		4:00 PM	
8:00 AM		4:30 PM	
8:30 AM		5:00 PM	
9:00 AM		5:30 PM	
9:30 AM		6:00 PM	
10:00 AM		6:30 PM	
10:30 AM		7:00 PM	
11:00 AM		7:30 PM	
11:30 AM		8:00 PM	
12:00 PM		8:30 PM	
12:30 PM		9:00 PM	
1:00 PM		9:30 PM	

WEEKS 41 – 42 PROGRESS

WEEK #__	MON	TUE	WED	THU	FRI	SAT	SUN
HEART: SEARCH & RESCUE							
Soul in Purgatory - Indulgence							
Soul for Deeper Conversion							
Day's Petitions - Pio Prayer							
SOUL: INTERIOR LIFE							
Morning Offering							
Mental Prayer							
Spiritual Reading							
Holy Mass							
Angelus (Regina Coeli)							
Holy Rosary							
Examination of Conscience							
MIND: SPIRITUAL READING							
Prep for Total Consecration							
Catholic Lifetime Reading Plan							
Other:							
STRENGTH: HEALTH/FITNESS							
Daily Workout Goals							
Daily Dietary Goals							

WEEK #__	MON	TUE	WED	THU	FRI	SAT	SUN
HEART: SEARCH & RESCUE							
Soul in Purgatory - Indulgence							
Soul for Deeper Conversion							
Day's Petitions - Pio Prayer							
SOUL: INTERIOR LIFE							
Morning Offering							
Mental Prayer							
Spiritual Reading							
Holy Mass							
Angelus (Regina Coeli)							
Holy Rosary							
Examination of Conscience							
MIND: SPIRITUAL READING							
Prep for Total Consecration							
Catholic Lifetime Reading Plan							
Other:							
STRENGTH: HEALTH/FITNESS							
Daily Workout Goals							
Daily Dietary Goals							

WEEKS 43 - 44 GOALS

"You shall love the Lord your God with all your heart, and with all your soul, and with all your mind, and with all your strength" (Mark 12:30).

HEART GOALS	SOUL GOALS

MIND GOALS	STRENGTH GOALS

THE DAILY PLAN

5:00 AM		1:30 PM	
5:30 AM		2:00 PM	
6:00 AM		2:30 PM	
6:30 AM		3:00 PM	
7:00 AM		3:30 PM	
7:30 AM		4:00 PM	
8:00 AM		4:30 PM	
8:30 AM		5:00 PM	
9:00 AM		5:30 PM	
9:30 AM		6:00 PM	
10:00 AM		6:30 PM	
10:30 AM		7:00 PM	
11:00 AM		7:30 PM	
11:30 AM		8:00 PM	
12:00 PM		8:30 PM	
12:30 PM		9:00 PM	
1:00 PM		9:30 PM	

WEEKS 43 – 44 PROGRESS

WEEK #__	MON	TUE	WED	THU	FRI	SAT	SUN
HEART: SEARCH & RESCUE							
Soul in Purgatory - Indulgence							
Soul for Deeper Conversion							
Day's Petitions - Pio Prayer							
SOUL: INTERIOR LIFE							
Morning Offering							
Mental Prayer							
Spiritual Reading							
Holy Mass							
Angelus (Regina Coeli)							
Holy Rosary							
Examination of Conscience							
MIND: SPIRITUAL READING							
Prep for Total Consecration							
Catholic Lifetime Reading Plan							
Other:							
STRENGTH: HEALTH/FITNESS							
Daily Workout Goals							
Daily Dietary Goals							

WEEK #__	MON	TUE	WED	THU	FRI	SAT	SUN
HEART: SEARCH & RESCUE							
Soul in Purgatory - Indulgence							
Soul for Deeper Conversion							
Day's Petitions - Pio Prayer							
SOUL: INTERIOR LIFE							
Morning Offering							
Mental Prayer							
Spiritual Reading							
Holy Mass							
Angelus (Regina Coeli)							
Holy Rosary							
Examination of Conscience							
MIND: SPIRITUAL READING							
Prep for Total Consecration							
Catholic Lifetime Reading Plan							
Other:							
STRENGTH: HEALTH/FITNESS							
Daily Workout Goals							
Daily Dietary Goals							

WEEKS 45 - 46 GOALS

"You shall love the Lord your God with all your heart, and with all your soul, and with all your mind, and with all your strength" (Mark 12:30).

HEART GOALS	SOUL GOALS

MIND GOALS	STRENGTH GOALS

THE DAILY PLAN

5:00 AM		1:30 PM	
5:30 AM		2:00 PM	
6:00 AM		2:30 PM	
6:30 AM		3:00 PM	
7:00 AM		3:30 PM	
7:30 AM		4:00 PM	
8:00 AM		4:30 PM	
8:30 AM		5:00 PM	
9:00 AM		5:30 PM	
9:30 AM		6:00 PM	
10:00 AM		6:30 PM	
10:30 AM		7:00 PM	
11:00 AM		7:30 PM	
11:30 AM		8:00 PM	
12:00 PM		8:30 PM	
12:30 PM		9:00 PM	
1:00 PM		9:30 PM	

WEEKS 45 – 46 PROGRESS

WEEK #__	MON	TUE	WED	THU	FRI	SAT	SUN
HEART: SEARCH & RESCUE							
Soul in Purgatory - Indulgence							
Soul for Deeper Conversion							
Day's Petitions - Pio Prayer							
SOUL: INTERIOR LIFE							
Morning Offering							
Mental Prayer							
Spiritual Reading							
Holy Mass							
Angelus (Regina Coeli)							
Holy Rosary							
Examination of Conscience							
MIND: SPIRITUAL READING							
Prep for Total Consecration							
Catholic Lifetime Reading Plan							
Other:							
STRENGTH: HEALTH/FITNESS							
Daily Workout Goals							
Daily Dietary Goals							

WEEK #__	MON	TUE	WED	THU	FRI	SAT	SUN
HEART: SEARCH & RESCUE							
Soul in Purgatory - Indulgence							
Soul for Deeper Conversion							
Day's Petitions - Pio Prayer							
SOUL: INTERIOR LIFE							
Morning Offering							
Mental Prayer							
Spiritual Reading							
Holy Mass							
Angelus (Regina Coeli)							
Holy Rosary							
Examination of Conscience							
MIND: SPIRITUAL READING							
Prep for Total Consecration							
Catholic Lifetime Reading Plan							
Other:							
STRENGTH: HEALTH/FITNESS							
Daily Workout Goals							
Daily Dietary Goals							

WEEKS 47 - 48 GOALS

"You shall love the Lord your God with all your heart, and with all your soul, and with all your mind, and with all your strength" (Mark 12:30).

HEART GOALS	SOUL GOALS

MIND GOALS	STRENGTH GOALS

THE DAILY PLAN			
5:00 AM		1:30 PM	
5:30 AM		2:00 PM	
6:00 AM		2:30 PM	
6:30 AM		3:00 PM	
7:00 AM		3:30 PM	
7:30 AM		4:00 PM	
8:00 AM		4:30 PM	
8:30 AM		5:00 PM	
9:00 AM		5:30 PM	
9:30 AM		6:00 PM	
10:00 AM		6:30 PM	
10:30 AM		7:00 PM	
11:00 AM		7:30 PM	
11:30 AM		8:00 PM	
12:00 PM		8:30 PM	
12:30 PM		9:00 PM	
1:00 PM		9:30 PM	

WEEKS 47 – 48 PROGRESS

WEEK #__	MON	TUE	WED	THU	FRI	SAT	SUN
HEART: SEARCH & RESCUE							
Soul in Purgatory - Indulgence							
Soul for Deeper Conversion							
Day's Petitions - Pio Prayer							
SOUL: INTERIOR LIFE							
Morning Offering							
Mental Prayer							
Spiritual Reading							
Holy Mass							
Angelus (Regina Coeli)							
Holy Rosary							
Examination of Conscience							
MIND: SPIRITUAL READING							
Prep for Total Consecration							
Catholic Lifetime Reading Plan							
Other:							
STRENGTH: HEALTH/FITNESS							
Daily Workout Goals							
Daily Dietary Goals							

WEEK #__	MON	TUE	WED	THU	FRI	SAT	SUN
HEART: SEARCH & RESCUE							
Soul in Purgatory - Indulgence							
Soul for Deeper Conversion							
Day's Petitions - Pio Prayer							
SOUL: INTERIOR LIFE							
Morning Offering							
Mental Prayer							
Spiritual Reading							
Holy Mass							
Angelus (Regina Coeli)							
Holy Rosary							
Examination of Conscience							
MIND: SPIRITUAL READING							
Prep for Total Consecration							
Catholic Lifetime Reading Plan							
Other:							
STRENGTH: HEALTH/FITNESS							
Daily Workout Goals							
Daily Dietary Goals							

WEEKS 49 - 50 GOALS

"You shall love the Lord your God with all your heart, and with all your soul, and with all your mind, and with all your strength" (Mark 12:30).

HEART GOALS	SOUL GOALS

MIND GOALS	STRENGTH GOALS

THE DAILY PLAN			
5:00 AM		1:30 PM	
5:30 AM		2:00 PM	
6:00 AM		2:30 PM	
6:30 AM		3:00 PM	
7:00 AM		3:30 PM	
7:30 AM		4:00 PM	
8:00 AM		4:30 PM	
8:30 AM		5:00 PM	
9:00 AM		5:30 PM	
9:30 AM		6:00 PM	
10:00 AM		6:30 PM	
10:30 AM		7:00 PM	
11:00 AM		7:30 PM	
11:30 AM		8:00 PM	
12:00 PM		8:30 PM	
12:30 PM		9:00 PM	
1:00 PM		9:30 PM	

WEEKS 49 – 50 PROGRESS

WEEK #__	MON	TUE	WED	THU	FRI	SAT	SUN
HEART: SEARCH & RESCUE							
Soul in Purgatory - Indulgence							
Soul for Deeper Conversion							
Day's Petitions - Pio Prayer							
SOUL: INTERIOR LIFE							
Morning Offering							
Mental Prayer							
Spiritual Reading							
Holy Mass							
Angelus (Regina Coeli)							
Holy Rosary							
Examination of Conscience							
MIND: SPIRITUAL READING							
Prep for Total Consecration							
Catholic Lifetime Reading Plan							
Other:							
STRENGTH: HEALTH/FITNESS							
Daily Workout Goals							
Daily Dietary Goals							

WEEK #__	MON	TUE	WED	THU	FRI	SAT	SUN
HEART: SEARCH & RESCUE							
Soul in Purgatory - Indulgence							
Soul for Deeper Conversion							
Day's Petitions - Pio Prayer							
SOUL: INTERIOR LIFE							
Morning Offering							
Mental Prayer							
Spiritual Reading							
Holy Mass							
Angelus (Regina Coeli)							
Holy Rosary							
Examination of Conscience							
MIND: SPIRITUAL READING							
Prep for Total Consecration							
Catholic Lifetime Reading Plan							
Other:							
STRENGTH: HEALTH/FITNESS							
Daily Workout Goals							
Daily Dietary Goals							

WEEKS 51 - 52 GOALS

"You shall love the Lord your God with all your heart, and with all your soul, and with all your mind, and with all your strength" (Mark 12:30).

HEART GOALS	SOUL GOALS

MIND GOALS	STRENGTH GOALS

THE DAILY PLAN			
5:00 AM		1:30 PM	
5:30 AM		2:00 PM	
6:00 AM		2:30 PM	
6:30 AM		3:00 PM	
7:00 AM		3:30 PM	
7:30 AM		4:00 PM	
8:00 AM		4:30 PM	
8:30 AM		5:00 PM	
9:00 AM		5:30 PM	
9:30 AM		6:00 PM	
10:00 AM		6:30 PM	
10:30 AM		7:00 PM	
11:00 AM		7:30 PM	
11:30 AM		8:00 PM	
12:00 PM		8:30 PM	
12:30 PM		9:00 PM	
1:00 PM		9:30 PM	

WEEKS 51 – 52 PROGRESS

WEEK #___	MON	TUE	WED	THU	FRI	SAT	SUN
HEART: SEARCH & RESCUE							
Soul in Purgatory - Indulgence							
Soul for Deeper Conversion							
Day's Petitions - Pio Prayer							
SOUL: INTERIOR LIFE							
Morning Offering							
Mental Prayer							
Spiritual Reading							
Holy Mass							
Angelus (Regina Coeli)							
Holy Rosary							
Examination of Conscience							
MIND: SPIRITUAL READING							
Prep for Total Consecration							
Catholic Lifetime Reading Plan							
Other:							
STRENGTH: HEALTH/FITNESS							
Daily Workout Goals							
Daily Dietary Goals							

WEEK #___	MON	TUE	WED	THU	FRI	SAT	SUN
HEART: SEARCH & RESCUE							
Soul in Purgatory - Indulgence							
Soul for Deeper Conversion							
Day's Petitions - Pio Prayer							
SOUL: INTERIOR LIFE							
Morning Offering							
Mental Prayer							
Spiritual Reading							
Holy Mass							
Angelus (Regina Coeli)							
Holy Rosary							
Examination of Conscience							
MIND: SPIRITUAL READING							
Prep for Total Consecration							
Catholic Lifetime Reading Plan							
Other:							
STRENGTH: HEALTH/FITNESS							
Daily Workout Goals							
Daily Dietary Goals							

SAINTS TO INTERCEDE FOR HOLY SOULS AND COMRADES

A-TEAM SAINTS

- ❑ St. Mary
- ❑ St. Joseph
- ❑ St. Anne
- ❑ St. Joachim
- ❑ St. Michael the Archangel
- ❑ St. Raphael the Archangel
- ❑ St. Gabriel the Archangel

APOSTLES

- ❑ St. Andrew
- ❑ St. Bartholomew
- ❑ St. James the Greater
- ❑ St. James the Less
- ❑ St. John the Evangelist
- ❑ St. Jude
- ❑ St. Matthew
- ❑ St. Matthias
- ❑ St. Peter
- ❑ St. Philip
- ❑ St. Simon
- ❑ St. Thomas

FATHERS OF THE CHURCH

- ❑ St. Alexander
- ❑ St. Barnabas
- ❑ St. Clement of Alexandria
- ❑ St. Clement of Rome
- ❑ St. Cyprian
- ❑ St. Dionysius of Rome
- ❑ St. Ephraim the Syrian
- ❑ St. Gregory Nyssa
- ❑ St. Gregory Thaumaturgus
- ❑ St. Hippolytus
- ❑ St. Ignatius of Antioch
- ❑ St. Irenaeus
- ❑ St. John of Damascus
- ❑ St. Justin Martyr
- ❑ St. Methodius
- ❑ St. Pamphilus

- ❑ St. Papias
- ❑ St. Peter of Alexandria
- ❑ St. Polycarp of Smyrna
- ❑ St. Victorinus
- ❑ St. Vincent of Lerins

DOCTORS OF THE CHURCH

- ❑ St. Ambrose
- ❑ St. Jerome
- ❑ St. Augustine of Hippo
- ❑ St. Gregory the Great
- ❑ St. Athanasius
- ❑ St. Basil the Great
- ❑ St. Gregory Nazianzus
- ❑ St. John Crystostom
- ❑ St. Ephraem
- ❑ St. Hilary of Poitiers
- ❑ St. Cyril of Jerusalem
- ❑ St. Cyril of Alexandria
- ❑ St. Leo the Great
- ❑ St. Peter Chrysologus
- ❑ St. Isidore
- ❑ St. Bede, the Venerable
- ❑ St. John Damascene
- ❑ St. Peter Damian
- ❑ St. Anselm
- ❑ St. Bernard of Clairvaux
- ❑ St. Anthony of Padua
- ❑ St. Albert the Great
- ❑ St. Bonaventure
- ❑ St. Thomas Aquinas
- ❑ St. Catherine of Siena
- ❑ St. Teresa of Jesus of Avila
- ❑ St. Peter Canisius
- ❑ St. John of the Cross
- ❑ St. Robert Bellarmine
- ❑ St. Lawrence of Brindisi
- ❑ St. Francis de Sales
- ❑ St. Alphonsus Ligouri
- ❑ St. Therese of Lisieux

❑ St. Hildegard of Bingen
❑ St. John of Avila

SAINTS REMEMBERED AT MASS
❑ St. Adalbert
❑ St. Aloysius Gonzaga
❑ St. Andrew Dung-Lac
❑ St. Ansgar
❑ St. Anthony Mary Zaccaria
❑ St. Anthony Mary Claret
❑ St. Apollinaris
❑ St. Augustine of Canterbury
❑ St. Augustine Zhao Rong
❑ St. Bernardine of Siena
❑ St. Boniface
❑ St. Cajetan
❑ St. Casmir
❑ St. Catherine of Alexandria
❑ St. Charles Borromeo
❑ St. Christoper Magallanes
❑ St. Columban
❑ St. Damien Joseph de Veuster
❑ St. Eusebius of Vercelli
❑ St. Frances Xavier Cabrini
❑ St. Francis of Paola
❑ St. Francis Xavier
❑ St. George
❑ St. Henry
❑ St. Ignatius of Loyola
❑ St. Isaac Jogues
❑ St. Jerome Emiliani
❑ St. John Baptist de la Salle
❑ St. John Eudes
❑ St. John Leonardi
❑ St. John of Capistrano
❑ St. John of God
❑ St. John of Kanty
❑ St. John the Baptist
❑ St. Joseph Calasanz
❑ St. Lawrence Ruiz
❑ St. Luke

❑ St. Margaret Mary Alacoque
❑ St. Mark
❑ St. Martha
❑ St. Mary Magdalene
❑ St. Norbert
❑ St. Paul
❑ St. Paul of the Cross
❑ St. Peter Claver
❑ St. Peter Julian Eymard
❑ St. Philip Neri
❑ St. Raymond of Penafort
❑ St. Rita of Cascia
❑ St. Romuald
❑ St. Rose Philippine Duchesne
❑ St. Scholastica
❑ St. Sharbel Makhluf
❑ St. Stanislaus
❑ St. Teresa Benedicta of the Cross
❑ St. Timothy
❑ St. Titus
❑ St. Toribio de Mongrovejo
❑ St. Vincent Ferrer
❑ St. Wenceslaus

LITANY OF THE SAINTS
❑ St. Agatha
❑ St. Agnes
❑ St. Anastasia
❑ St. Benedict
❑ St. Cecilia
❑ St. Clare
❑ St. Cosmos
❑ St. Damian
❑ St. Dominic
❑ St. Lucy
❑ St. Martin
❑ St. Nicholas
❑ St. Sebastian
❑ St. Stephen
❑ St. Vincent

POPULAR SAINTS
- ❑ St. Angela Merici
- ❑ St. Bernadette
- ❑ St. Christopher
- ❑ St. Dymphna
- ❑ St. Faustina
- ❑ St. Francis of Assisi
- ❑ St. Gerard Majella
- ❑ St. Joan of Arc
- ❑ St. John Bosco
- ❑ St. John Neumann
- ❑ St. John Vianney
- ❑ St. Juan Diego
- ❑ St. Katharine Drexel
- ❑ St. Louis de Montfort
- ❑ St. Martin de Porres
- ❑ St. Padre Pio
- ❑ St. Patrick
- ❑ St. Rose of Lima
- ❑ St. Thomas More
- ❑ St. Valentine
- ❑ St. Veronica

PATRON SAINTS OF HOLY SOULS IN PURGATORY
- ❑ St. Gertrude
- ❑ St. John Macias
- ❑ St. Nicholas of Tolentino
- ❑ St. Odilo

PATRON SAINTS AGAINST EVIL SPIRITS
- ❑ St. Agrippina
- ❑ St. Amabilis of Auvergne
- ❑ St. Andrew Avillino
- ❑ St. Bruno
- ❑ St. Cyriacus
- ❑ St. Demetrius of Sermium
- ❑ St. Deodatus of Nevers
- ❑ St. Josephat Kunsevich
- ❑ St. Lucian
- ❑ St. Lucy Bufalari
- ❑ St. Marcian
- ❑ St. Margaret of Antioch

- ❑ St. Margaret of Fontana
- ❑ St. Patroclus of Troyes
- ❑ St. Paulinus of Nola
- ❑ St. Quirinus
- ❑ St. Ubaldus Baldessini

INCORRUPTIBLES
- ❑ St. Charbel Makhlouf
- ❑ St. Josaphat
- ❑ St. Mary Magdalene de Pazzi
- ❑ St. Veronica Giulani
- ❑ St. Vincent de Paul
- ❑ St. Zita

MARTYRS
- ❑ St. Andrew Kim Taegon
- ❑ St. Blaise
- ❑ St. Charles Lwanga
- ❑ St. Claudius the Martyr
- ❑ St. Denis
- ❑ St. Dionysia the Martyr
- ❑ St. Felicity
- ❑ St. Fidelis of Sigmaringen
- ❑ St. Hilaria the Martyr
- ❑ St. Hippolytus of Rome
- ❑ St. Januarius
- ❑ St. Jason the Martyr
- ❑ St. Jean de Brebeuf
- ❑ St. John Fisher
- ❑ St. Lawrence of Rome
- ❑ St. Maria Goretti
- ❑ St. Maurus the Martyr
- ❑ St. Maximilian Kolbe
- ❑ St. Pancras
- ❑ St. Paul Chong Hasang
- ❑ St. Paul Miki
- ❑ St. Perpetua
- ❑ St. Peter Chanel
- ❑ St. Peter the Exorcist
- ❑ St. Polycarp
- ❑ St. Stanislaus
- ❑ St. Thomas Becket

SAINTS WHO WERE POPES

- ❑ St. Linus
- ❑ St. Anacletus
- ❑ St. Clement I
- ❑ St. Evaristus
- ❑ St. Alexander I
- ❑ St. Sixtus I
- ❑ St. Telesphorus
- ❑ St. Hyginus
- ❑ St. Pius I
- ❑ St. Anicetus
- ❑ St. Soter
- ❑ St. Eleutherius
- ❑ St. Victor I
- ❑ St. Zephyrinus
- ❑ St. Callistus I
- ❑ St. Urban I
- ❑ St. Pontain
- ❑ St. Anterus
- ❑ St. Fabian
- ❑ St. Cornelius
- ❑ St. Lucius I
- ❑ St. Stephen I
- ❑ St. Sixtus II
- ❑ St. Dionysius
- ❑ St. Felix I
- ❑ St. Eutychian
- ❑ St. Gaius
- ❑ St. Marcellinus
- ❑ St. Marcellus I
- ❑ St. Eusebius
- ❑ St. Miltiades
- ❑ St. Sylvester I
- ❑ St. Marcus
- ❑ St. Julius I
- ❑ St. Damasus I
- ❑ St. Siricius
- ❑ St. Anastasius I
- ❑ St. Innocent I
- ❑ St. Zosimus
- ❑ St. Boniface I
- ❑ St. Celestine I
- ❑ St. Sixtus III
- ❑ St. Hilarius
- ❑ St. Simplicius
- ❑ St. Felix III
- ❑ St. Gelasius I
- ❑ St. Anastasius II
- ❑ St. Symmachus
- ❑ St. Hormisdas
- ❑ St. John I
- ❑ St. Felix IV
- ❑ St. Agapetus I
- ❑ St. Silverius
- ❑ St. Boniface IV
- ❑ St. Deusdedit
- ❑ St. Martin I
- ❑ St. Eugene I
- ❑ St. Vitalian
- ❑ St. Agatho
- ❑ St. Leo II
- ❑ St. Benedict II
- ❑ St. Sergius I
- ❑ St. Gregory II
- ❑ St. Gregory III
- ❑ St. Zachary
- ❑ St. Paul I
- ❑ St. Leo III
- ❑ St. Paschal I
- ❑ St. Leo IV
- ❑ St. Nicholas I the Great
- ❑ St. Adrian III
- ❑ St. Leo IX
- ❑ St. Gregory VII
- ❑ St. Celestine V
- ❑ St. Pius V
- ❑ St. Pius X

SAINTS WHO WERE FATHERS

- ❏ St. Adauctus
- ❏ St. Alonso Rodriguez
- ❏ St. Andrew of Arezzo
- ❏ St. Ansfrid of Utrecht
- ❏ St. Arnulf of Metz
- ❏ St. Artemius of Rome
- ❏ St. Catervus
- ❏ St. Dagobert II
- ❏ St. Donivald
- ❏ St. Edgar the Peaceful
- ❏ St. Edwin of Northumbria
- ❏ St. Ethelbert of Kent
- ❏ St. Eucherius of Lyon
- ❏ St. Eustachius
- ❏ St. Fiace
- ❏ St. Fragan
- ❏ St. Francis Borgia
- ❏ St. Gabinus
- ❏ St. Gregory of Langres
- ❏ St. Gregory the Illuminator
- ❏ St. Hubert of Liege
- ❏ St. Isidore the Farmer
- ❏ St. John the Almoner
- ❏ St. Leopold III
- ❏ St. Louis IX
- ❏ St. Michael Kozaki
- ❏ St. Nicholas of Flüe
- ❏ St. Nilus the Elder
- ❏ St. Nilus the Younger
- ❏ St. Orentius of Loret
- ❏ St. Pacian of Barcelona
- ❏ St. Palmatius of Rome
- ❏ St. Pepin of Landen
- ❏ St. Peter Lieou
- ❏ St. Peter Orseolo
- ❏ St. Philip of Rome
- ❏ St. Pinian
- ❏ St. Quirinus the Jailer
- ❏ St. Simplicius of Bourges
- ❏ St. Solomon I
- ❏ St. Stephen of Hungary
- ❏ St. Vincent Madelgaire
- ❏ St. Vitalis of Milan
- ❏ St. Vladimir I of Kiev
- ❏ St. Walbert of Hainault
- ❏ St. Walfrid

SAINTS WHO WERE MOTHERS

- ❏ St. Agia
- ❏ St. Amalburga
- ❏ St. Amunia
- ❏ St. Bathilde
- ❏ St. Bridget of Sweden
- ❏ St. Candida of Rome
- ❏ St. Cecilia Yu Sosa
- ❏ St. Clotilde
- ❏ St. Crispina
- ❏ St. Elizabeth
- ❏ St. Elizabeth Ann Seton
- ❏ St. Felicity of Rome
- ❏ St. Frances of Rome
- ❏ St. Gianna Beretta Molla
- ❏ St. Gladys
- ❏ St. Gorgonia
- ❏ St. Gwen
- ❏ St. Hedwig of Andechs
- ❏ St. Helena
- ❏ St. Hildegund
- ❏ St. Humility
- ❏ St. Ida of Herzfeld
- ❏ St. Jacoba
- ❏ St. Jeanne de Chantal
- ❏ St. Judith of Prussia
- ❏ St. Ludmila
- ❏ St. Margaret of Cortona
- ❏ St. Margaret of Scotland
- ❏ St. Monica
- ❏ St. Natalia
- ❏ St. Non
- ❏ St. Nonna
- ❏ St. Olga of Kiev
- ❏ St. Patricia of Nicomedia
- ❏ St. Paula of Rome
- ❏ St. Priscilla of Rome
- ❏ St. Publia

- ☐ St. Rita of Cascia
- ☐ St. Saxburgh of Ely
- ☐ St. Sigrada
- ☐ St. Silvia of Rome
- ☐ St. Sophia
- ☐ St. Valeria of Milan
- ☐ St. Waltrude
- ☐ St. Wilfrida
- ☐ St. Zoe of Pamphylia

SAINTS WHO WERE CONVERTS

- ☐ St. Acestes
- ☐ St. Anne Line
- ☐ St. Audax
- ☐ St. Aurea
- ☐ St. Auxibius
- ☐ St. Barbara
- ☐ St. Camilla
- ☐ St. Craton
- ☐ St. Felicity of Carthage
- ☐ St. Gentian
- ☐ St. Gonzaga Gonza
- ☐ St. Henry Morse
- ☐ St. Irene
- ☐ St. James the Hermit
- ☐ St. John Ogilvie
- ☐ St. John Roberts
- ☐ St. Joseph Mukasa
- ☐ St. Joseph of Arimathea
- ☐ St. Josephine Bakhita
- ☐ St. Kieran
- ☐ St. Kizito
- ☐ St. Libert
- ☐ St. Martin of Tours
- ☐ St. Mathurin
- ☐ St. Mellon
- ☐ St. Odo the Good
- ☐ St. Olaf II
- ☐ St. Palatias
- ☐ St. Pancras of Rome
- ☐ St. Paulina of Rome
- ☐ St. Pelagia the Penitent
- ☐ St. Peter Ou

- ☐ St. Philip the Deacon
- ☐ St. Processus
- ☐ St. Ptolemy of Nepi
- ☐ St. Pudens of Rome
- ☐ St. Quentin
- ☐ St. Ralph Sherwin
- ☐ St. Regina
- ☐ St. Romanos the Melodist
- ☐ St. Romaric
- ☐ St. Romulus
- ☐ St. Sallustia
- ☐ St. Thamel
- ☐ St. Valeria of Limoges

OTHER SAINTS

- ☐ _____
- ☐ _____
- ☐ _____
- ☐ _____
- ☐ _____
- ☐ _____
- ☐ _____
- ☐ _____
- ☐ _____
- ☐ _____
- ☐ _____
- ☐ _____
- ☐ _____
- ☐ _____
- ☐ _____
- ☐ _____
- ☐ _____
- ☐ _____
- ☐ _____
- ☐ _____
- ☐ _____
- ☐ _____
- ☐ _____
- ☐ _____
- ☐ _____
- ☐ _____
- ☐ _____
- ☐ _____
- ☐ _____
- ☐ _____
- ☐ _____
- ☐ _____

OTHER SAINTS

- ☐ _____
- ☐ _____
- ☐ _____
- ☐ _____
- ☐ _____
- ☐ _____
- ☐ _____
- ☐ _____
- ☐ _____
- ☐ _____
- ☐ _____
- ☐ _____
- ☐ _____
- ☐ _____
- ☐ _____
- ☐ _____
- ☐ _____
- ☐ _____
- ☐ _____
- ☐ _____
- ☐ _____
- ☐ _____
- ☐ _____
- ☐ _____
- ☐ _____
- ☐ _____
- ☐ _____
- ☐ _____
- ☐ _____
- ☐ _____
- ☐ _____
- ☐ _____
- ☐ _____
- ☐ _____
- ☐ _____
- ☐ _____
- ☐ _____
- ☐ _____
- ☐ _____
- ☐ _____
- ☐ _____
- ☐ _____
- ☐ _____
- ☐ _____
- ☐ _____

OTHER SAINTS

- ☐ _____
- ☐ _____
- ☐ _____
- ☐ _____
- ☐ _____
- ☐ _____
- ☐ _____
- ☐ _____
- ☐ _____
- ☐ _____
- ☐ _____
- ☐ _____
- ☐ _____
- ☐ _____
- ☐ _____
- ☐ _____
- ☐ _____
- ☐ _____
- ☐ _____
- ☐ _____
- ☐ _____
- ☐ _____
- ☐ _____
- ☐ _____
- ☐ _____
- ☐ _____
- ☐ _____
- ☐ _____
- ☐ _____
- ☐ _____
- ☐ _____
- ☐ _____
- ☐ _____
- ☐ _____
- ☐ _____
- ☐ _____
- ☐ _____
- ☐ _____
- ☐ _____
- ☐ _____
- ☐ _____
- ☐ _____
- ☐ _____
- ☐ _____
- ☐ _____

OTHER SAINTS

☐ _____
☐ _____
☐ _____
☐ _____
☐ _____
☐ _____
☐ _____
☐ _____
☐ _____
☐ _____
☐ _____
☐ _____
☐ _____
☐ _____
☐ _____
☐ _____
☐ _____
☐ _____
☐ _____
☐ _____
☐ _____
☐ _____
☐ _____
☐ _____
☐ _____
☐ _____
☐ _____
☐ _____
☐ _____
☐ _____
☐ _____
☐ _____
☐ _____
☐ _____
☐ _____
☐ _____
☐ _____
☐ _____
☐ _____
☐ _____
☐ _____
☐ _____
☐ _____
☐ _____
☐ _____

OTHER SAINTS

☐ _____
☐ _____
☐ _____
☐ _____
☐ _____
☐ _____
☐ _____
☐ _____
☐ _____
☐ _____
☐ _____
☐ _____
☐ _____
☐ _____
☐ _____
☐ _____
☐ _____
☐ _____
☐ _____
☐ _____
☐ _____
☐ _____
☐ _____
☐ _____
☐ _____
☐ _____
☐ _____
☐ _____
☐ _____
☐ _____
☐ _____
☐ _____
☐ _____
☐ _____
☐ _____
☐ _____
☐ _____
☐ _____
☐ _____
☐ _____
☐ _____
☐ _____
☐ _____
☐ _____
☐ _____

HOLY SOULS IN PURGATORY
FOR WHOM TO PRAY

HOLY SOULS

☐ _____
☐ _____
☐ _____
☐ _____
☐ _____
☐ _____
☐ _____
☐ _____
☐ _____
☐ _____
☐ _____
☐ _____
☐ _____
☐ _____
☐ _____
☐ _____
☐ _____
☐ _____
☐ _____
☐ _____
☐ _____
☐ _____
☐ _____
☐ _____
☐ _____
☐ _____
☐ _____
☐ _____
☐ _____
☐ _____
☐ _____
☐ _____
☐ _____
☐ _____
☐ _____
☐ _____
☐ _____

HOLY SOULS

☐ _____
☐ _____
☐ _____
☐ _____
☐ _____
☐ _____
☐ _____
☐ _____
☐ _____
☐ _____
☐ _____
☐ _____
☐ _____
☐ _____
☐ _____
☐ _____
☐ _____
☐ _____
☐ _____
☐ _____
☐ _____
☐ _____
☐ _____
☐ _____
☐ _____
☐ _____
☐ _____
☐ _____
☐ _____
☐ _____
☐ _____
☐ _____
☐ _____
☐ _____
☐ _____
☐ _____
☐ _____

HOLY SOULS

- ☐ _____
- ☐ _____
- ☐ _____
- ☐ _____
- ☐ _____
- ☐ _____
- ☐ _____
- ☐ _____
- ☐ _____
- ☐ _____
- ☐ _____
- ☐ _____
- ☐ _____
- ☐ _____
- ☐ _____
- ☐ _____
- ☐ _____
- ☐ _____
- ☐ _____
- ☐ _____
- ☐ _____
- ☐ _____
- ☐ _____
- ☐ _____
- ☐ _____
- ☐ _____
- ☐ _____
- ☐ _____
- ☐ _____
- ☐ _____
- ☐ _____
- ☐ _____
- ☐ _____
- ☐ _____
- ☐ _____
- ☐ _____
- ☐ _____
- ☐ _____
- ☐ _____
- ☐ _____
- ☐ _____
- ☐ _____
- ☐ _____

HOLY SOULS

- ☐ _____
- ☐ _____
- ☐ _____
- ☐ _____
- ☐ _____
- ☐ _____
- ☐ _____
- ☐ _____
- ☐ _____
- ☐ _____
- ☐ _____
- ☐ _____
- ☐ _____
- ☐ _____
- ☐ _____
- ☐ _____
- ☐ _____
- ☐ _____
- ☐ _____
- ☐ _____
- ☐ _____
- ☐ _____
- ☐ _____
- ☐ _____
- ☐ _____
- ☐ _____
- ☐ _____
- ☐ _____
- ☐ _____
- ☐ _____
- ☐ _____
- ☐ _____
- ☐ _____
- ☐ _____
- ☐ _____
- ☐ _____
- ☐ _____
- ☐ _____
- ☐ _____
- ☐ _____
- ☐ _____
- ☐ _____
- ☐ _____

HOLY SOULS

❑ _____
❑ _____
❑ _____
❑ _____
❑ _____
❑ _____
❑ _____
❑ _____
❑ _____
❑ _____
❑ _____
❑ _____
❑ _____
❑ _____
❑ _____
❑ _____
❑ _____
❑ _____
❑ _____
❑ _____
❑ _____
❑ _____
❑ _____
❑ _____
❑ _____
❑ _____
❑ _____
❑ _____
❑ _____
❑ _____
❑ _____
❑ _____
❑ _____
❑ _____
❑ _____
❑ _____
❑ _____
❑ _____
❑ _____
❑ _____
❑ _____

HOLY SOULS

❑ _____
❑ _____
❑ _____
❑ _____
❑ _____
❑ _____
❑ _____
❑ _____
❑ _____
❑ _____
❑ _____
❑ _____
❑ _____
❑ _____
❑ _____
❑ _____
❑ _____
❑ _____
❑ _____
❑ _____
❑ _____
❑ _____
❑ _____
❑ _____
❑ _____
❑ _____
❑ _____
❑ _____
❑ _____
❑ _____
❑ _____
❑ _____
❑ _____
❑ _____
❑ _____
❑ _____
❑ _____
❑ _____
❑ _____
❑ _____
❑ _____

HOLY SOULS

- ☐ _____
- ☐ _____
- ☐ _____
- ☐ _____
- ☐ _____
- ☐ _____
- ☐ _____
- ☐ _____
- ☐ _____
- ☐ _____
- ☐ _____
- ☐ _____
- ☐ _____
- ☐ _____
- ☐ _____
- ☐ _____
- ☐ _____
- ☐ _____
- ☐ _____
- ☐ _____
- ☐ _____
- ☐ _____
- ☐ _____
- ☐ _____
- ☐ _____
- ☐ _____
- ☐ _____
- ☐ _____
- ☐ _____
- ☐ _____
- ☐ _____
- ☐ _____
- ☐ _____
- ☐ _____
- ☐ _____
- ☐ _____
- ☐ _____
- ☐ _____
- ☐ _____
- ☐ _____

HOLY SOULS

- ☐ _____
- ☐ _____
- ☐ _____
- ☐ _____
- ☐ _____
- ☐ _____
- ☐ _____
- ☐ _____
- ☐ _____
- ☐ _____
- ☐ _____
- ☐ _____
- ☐ _____
- ☐ _____
- ☐ _____
- ☐ _____
- ☐ _____
- ☐ _____
- ☐ _____
- ☐ _____
- ☐ _____
- ☐ _____
- ☐ _____
- ☐ _____
- ☐ _____
- ☐ _____
- ☐ _____
- ☐ _____
- ☐ _____
- ☐ _____
- ☐ _____
- ☐ _____
- ☐ _____
- ☐ _____
- ☐ _____
- ☐ _____
- ☐ _____
- ☐ _____
- ☐ _____
- ☐ _____

CITATIONS

[1] Pope Paul VI, *Indulgentiarum doctrina*, Apostolic Constitution, Chapter 2, Number 5.

[2] Pope John Paul II, Ad Limina meeting with American Bishops Region X, Number 5, 22 May 2004.

[3] *Primer on Indulgences*, Catholic Answers, <http://www.catholic.com/tracts/primer-on-indulgences> Accessed 9 May 2012.

[4] Kellmeyer, Steve, *The Beauty of Grace Calendar of Indulgences 2012*, Bridegroom Press, Plano, Texas, 2012. Available through BridegroomPress.com.

[5] Ibid.

[6] McCloskey, Fr. John, "The Seven Daily Habits of Holy Apostolic People," *CatholiCity*. <http://www.catholicity.com/mccloskey/sevenhabits.html> Accessed 9 May 2012.

[7] Ibid.

[8] St. Josemaria Escriva, *The Way*, Chapter 6, Number 191.

[9] St. Josemaria Escriva, *The Way*, Chapter 3, Number 116.

[10] St. Josemaria Escriva, *Furrow*, Chapter 14, Number 474.

[11] McCloskey, Fr. John, Ibid.

[12] St. Faustina, Diary, 187.

[13] Partners in Evangelism, "The Power of Intercessory Prayer," The Word Among Us Inc., Ijamsville, MD, 21754 <http://www.christlife.org/resources/articles/IntercessoryPrayer.html> Accessed 17 May 2012.

[14] Pope John Paul II, Homily at the Canonization of St. Josemaria Escriva de Balaguer, 6 October 2002. Paragraphs 4-5.

[15] Second Vatican Ecumenical Council, *Gaudium et Spes*, 14.

Made in United States
North Haven, CT
24 March 2023

34482551R00104